THREE THOUSAND ORIGINAL EPIGRAMS

THE EPIGRAM BEING DEFINED
AS A SHORT WITTY POEM

by

John Pemberton

Published 2015 by arima publishing

ISBN 978 1 84549 651 7

Copyright © 2015 John Pemberton

10 Raven Way
Christchurch
Dorset
BH23 4BQ

tel: 01425 273632
email: jpemberton@ntlworld.com

The right of John Pemberton to be identified as the author of this work has been asserted in accordance with Sections 77 and 78 of the Copyright, Designs and Patents Act 1988.

All rights reserved.

This book is copyright. Subject to statutory exception and to provisions of relevant collective licensing agreements, no part of this publication may be reproduced, stored in a retrieval system, or transmitted in any form or by any means, without the prior written permission of the author.

Printed and bound in the United Kingdom

This book is sold subject to the conditions that it shall not, by way of trade or otherwise, be lent, re-sold, hired out, or otherwise circulated without the publisher's prior consent in any form of binding or cover other than that which it is published and without a similar condition including this condition being imposed on the subsequent purchaser.

arima publishing
ASK House, Northgate Avenue
Bury St Edmunds, Suffolk IP32 6BB
t: (+44) 01284 700321

www.arimapublishing.com

To

Joyce

Martin & Sue

CONTENTS

Chapter 1	Pages	1-7	Adolescence
Chapter 2	Pages	8-15	Ageing
Chapter 3	Pages	16-18	Ambition & Jobs
Chapter 4	Pages	19-20	Appearance
Chapter 5	Pages	21-23	Art
Chapter 6	Pages	24-38	Behaviour
Chapter 7	Pages	39-44	Business
Chapter 8	Pages	45-46	Celebrity & Fame
Chapter 9	Pages	47-54	Concepts
Chapter 10	Pages	55-58	Education
Chapter 11	Page>	59->>	Environment
Chapter 12	Pages	60-66	Epitaphs
Chapter 13	Pages	67-79	Fauna & Flora
Chapter 14	Pages	80-86	Food & Drink
Chapter 15	Pages	87-89	Friendship
Chapter 16	Pages	90-92	Genetics
Chapter 17	Pages	93-98	Government
Chapter 18	Pages	99-103	Health
Chapter 19	Pages	104-107	History
Chapter 20	Pages	108-109	Hobbies
Chapter 21	Pages	110-112	Holidays
Chapter 22	Pages	113-114	Hope & Emotions
Chapter 23	Pages	115-116	Humankind
Chapter 24	Pages	117-134	Humour
Chapter 25	Pages	135-137	Info-Tech
Chapter 26	Pages	138-145	Language
Chapter 27	Pages	146-149	Law
Chapter 28	Pages	150-156	Life
Chapter 29	Pages	157-169	Lifestyle
Chapter 30	Pages	170-173	Literature
Chapter 31	Pages	174-188	Love & Marriage
Chapter 32	Pages	189-192	Media
Chapter 33	Pages	193-197	Money Matters
Chapter 34	Pages	198-200	Music
Chapter 35	Pages	201-203	Nationality
Chapter 36	Pages	204-224	Nifty Lines
Chapter 37	Pages	225-245	Odd Extracts

CONTENTS cont'd

Chapter 38	Pages	246-249	On Reflection
Chapter 39	Pages	250-258	Poetry
Chapter 40	Pages	259-266	Queries
Chapter 41	Pages	267-268	Religion
Chapter 42	Pages	269-271	Science
Chapter 43	Pages	272-273	Seasons
Chapter 44	Pages	274-279	Sport
Chapter 45	Pages	280-282	Theatre
Chapter 46	Pages	283-295	Tips & Wrinkles
Chapter 47	Pages	296-319	To Ponder
Chapter 48	Pages	320-323	Transport
Chapter 49	Pages	324-326	War
Chapter 50	Pages	327-329	Weather
Chapter 51	Pages	330-338	Bonus Miscellany

Note: Chapter 11 has only one page.

PREAMBLE

The book comprises in excess of three thousand poems, each with a title and two lines of text. It is only on very few occasions that pure rhyme has not been used, leaving such as alliteration and assonance to be brought into play.

The number of poems per chapter ranges from 8 to 238, with the former filling just a single page and the latter no fewer than two dozen.

No matter your whereabouts there's a likelihood of a poem making you stop to think about what you've just read. Here are a few that might suit.

Chapter 1, page 5
Playtime
When children indulge in what we call playing,
It's practical learning they're blithely displaying.

Chapter 5, page 23
Objects of Art
Most objects of art created by man,
Tend to live longer than any man can.

Chapter 21, page 107
Picture Postcards
All postcards we send, and those we receive,
Have bright blue skies we can hardly believe.

Chapter 31, page 182
Love and Marriage
True love's a balance with equal weights
And marriage a truce where neither dictates.

Chapter 44, page 274

(Forgive me for rounding off with this one.)
All-round Sportsman
Whoever it was invented the ball
Was surely the greatest sportsman of all!

CHAPTER 1 with 61 two-liners

ADOLESCENCE

Adolescence
Adolescence determines how we grow up:
Whether just a mug or a saucer and cup.

Beach
The beach is a playground where children can run
And parents protect them from dangerous sun.

Behaviour
A child that's minded to have its own way
Might need reminding life isn't all play.

Best Behaviour
Children displaying delightful behaviour
Seem to be doing their parents a favour.

Bikes
When trials of youth become unforgiving,
Bikes can add new horizons to living.

Brother Bother
It seems big sister's phoning and flirting
Is more than a little bit disconcerting.

Children
Some mothers have children who frequently cry,
Which creates bad effects on most passers-by.

Childrens' Birthdays
Young children are always eager to find
What's inside wrappings they're leaving behind.

Coastal Sands
When youngsters are playing in coastal sands,
It's granular rock they mould with their hands.

Concern
No sooner they're weaned than little girls learn
What benefits flow from showing concern.

Crawlers
Most babies choose crawling on hands and knees;
But all, in the end, find roots for their feet.

Cred
Prior to buying a product on credit,
The young have to check how decent its cred is.

Credulity
Youngsters explore the age of naivety,
Readily thriving on youth's credulity.

Defence
Should sudden danger a child befall,
It coils itself like a foetal ball.

Doubting
When young we meekly believe what we're told,
But knowledge breeds doubting as years unfold.

Eager Sweethearts
Eager young sweethearts, both girls and boys,
Can seem to act like each others' toys.

Early Warning
The kid on his trike and the chic looking shy
Might one day marry, not knowing quite why.

Eighteen
Having reached eighteen and now fully grown,
You'll find a new world you can call your own.

Endless Questions
My endless questions, I always was told,
Would all be answered when I became old.

Endless Waiting
As no text message came and he didn't stop by,
She sat waiting in vain with her eyes never dry.

Free Rein
When children are told they can do as they choose,
More likely than not they'll just stand there bemused.

Funtime
Still to encounter life's problems to come,
It's mainly the young think living is fun.

Giveaway
A parrot can give the game away;
A child can, too. So mind what you say!

Growing Older
Be sure, young chap, it'll happen to you:
The older you grow the more you can't do.

Handed Down
When, languidly, youngsters declare 'I'm bored,'
The words haven't formed of their own accord.

Happy Hours
We smile when we hear small children at play;
If only their happiness came to stay!

Innocence
In our innocent days the faces we see
Return our smiles with innocence equally.

Jumble Sale
One day, surprised by a visiting male,
Her room had the look of a jumble sale.

Kids
With the din from the kids next door so amazing,
We've been forced to install some more triple glazing.

Kids and Dogs
Once, children were taught to be seen not heard;
Now, it's kids and dogs whose din is preferred.

Lads
Lads in teen years countermand
What their parentage had planned.

Learning Years
Our tender years are the learning years,
When memory captures all that it hears.

Little Darlings
Little darlings of three, one usually finds,
Like making it clear they've acquired their own minds.

Loofah
The loofah's a fibrous topical fruit
That kids in the bath will always dispute.

Mimics
Children appear not to listen to parents,
But always adopt their language and cadence.

Modern Miss
Sprawled on the sofa, her mobile to hand,
She yearns for the call they'd earlier planned.

Names
Names anxiously shouted when youngsters vanish
Are seldom common, more often outlandish.

New Learners
While new-born successors have plenty to learn,
To judge by their smiles it's of little concern.

Parental Mantra
Young adults will choose to go where the action is,
Expecting that parents will mind their own business.

Playtime
When children indulge in what we call playing,
It's practical learning they're blithely displaying.

Potent Youth
When potent youth has filled the stage,
Celebrate life's pubescent age.

Pubescence
As itching below becomes disturbing,
That's when you know your pubes are emerging.

Pushchair Baby
A pushchair baby sees where it's going,
Smiling at people, mummy unknowing.

Rebellious Youth
Whenever we speak of rebellious youth,
We might only refer to part of the truth.

Recovery
In a trice a child can turn happy from sad;
If only we all could recover like that!

Remnants
Among all the clutter that children acquire
There's sure to be remnants of cherished attire.

Santa
When Santa flies by on Christmas Eve,
A small child hopes there's something he'll leave.

Sewing Box
With children around, mum's sewing box sits
Prepared for odd things she'll happily fix.

Shouting Kids
When some things are banned and others allowed,
No wonder young kids keep shouting out loud.

Sibling Stress
Life's hard for a child who's awaiting a sibling,
And harder still when that sibling starts squabbling.

Teenage
Our teenage stage is filled with disguising,
Choosing, resisting, trying, surprising.

Teenagers
When teenagers challenge parental powers,
'Immediately' covers a couple of hours.

Teens
Politely said, each teen enjoys
The nightly toys of girls and boys.

Thumbs Up
Clearly, sweet baby, you find it great fun,
But, please, do try to stop sucking your thumb.

Toddler Talk
When toddlers fall we croon 'Oops a daisy.'
To all but the small, that's blooming crazy.

Uncles and Aunties
Aunties and uncles are popular guests:
They always comply with children's requests.

Urges
Youths are infused with the urges of men;
Rightly declined are their overtures, then.

Watch and Learn
If you want your offspring to wear your shoes,
Then 'Watch and Learn' is the motto to use.

Young Men
Almost every young man who's lived through his teens
Will tell you it's really as bad as it seems.

Youth
All elders know the strength and stress
Of youth's first urge we'd once possess.

Youth's Concern
Youth is concerned with its need to impose
A new independence as confidence grows.

CHAPTER 2 with 73 2-liners

AGEING

Acknowledged
Knowledge accumulates in the wizened,
Where it deteriorates, self-imprisoned.

Ageing
Most of us know when we're getting old;
Only the foolish need to be told.

Ageing Admission
An actress admits as the years flit by
Much more on make-up she's forced to rely.

Ageing Sages
Adding a year to one's earlier age
Ushers one nearer becoming a sage.

Anecdotage
Aware of repeating the same old stories,
He'd boast of achieving his anecdotage.

Anniversaries
Each anniversary serves
To keep account of our years.

Any Excuse
'It wasn't my fault', Mrs Smith maintained.
'My memory mislaid my name', she explained.

Being Old
When you have to concede to being old,
At least you don't need to do as you're told.

Birthday Numbers
Do not let birthday numbers rule your span
But measure what's of value while you can.

Chat Shop
When the oldies go to a barber's shop,
It's mostly for chat and partly for chop.

Comfort
Only the pensioner understands
Comfort demands clean feet and warm hands.

Covetings
Things we would covet when we were younger
Gave way each year to a different hunger.

Decrepitude
Decrepitude hovers over the old,
Despairing of health and fearing the cold.

Defaulting
Our faculties fail old burdens we'd shoulder,
But *we* aren't to blame for our growing older.

Dozing Time
The shorter our span of time has to run,
The longer our hours of dozing become.

Dreams and Means
Beyond the elderly lady's dreams
Are chosen bargains within her means.

Earthly Rebirths
When mothers retire they turn to earth's
Early seeding for perennial rebirths.

Eighties Mobility
Once eighties mobility takes its toll,
Logistical planning assumes a role.

Eightieth Birthday
On his eightieth birthday he sat chilling out,
Just wondering what all the fuss was about.

Elderly Pondering
While the elderly ponder on names they forgot,
Words like someone and somewhere are used quite a lot.

Energy
Ineluctably, energy lessens with age;
The effect affects equally lover and sage.

Ephemera
Collected ephemera help us recall
The things we'd forgotten from when we were small.

Extenuation
The older person's extenuation
Needs more frequent recuperation.

Eyesight
Our weakening eyes improve the view
Of younger faces that older grew.

Fantasy
He reckons to be both older and wiser;
The records agree he's a fantasizer.

Fatigue
When older folk finish what was required,
Achievement reveals them increasingly tired.

Fiftieth
It's not long since people have opted for fifty
To celebrate years that have flown by too swiftly.

Grandad
A grandchild arrived to great celebration,
Conferring on him a grand appellation!

Grandchildren
While grandparents hope they'll not be disturbed,
The grandchildren shout to make themselves heard.

Grandson
If I could still do what my grandson does,
Amazement would show in the both of us.

Growing
Growing old we can't refuse:
Growing up's for us to choose.

Hairs
The moment you learn you're of lessening years
Is when you start plucking hairs from your ears.

House Wise
Once eighties' mobility takes its toll,
Logistical planning assumes a role.

Hugs and Cuddles
Long gone are the days when hugs and cuddles
Could sooth away our worrisome troubles.

Ignoring Things
When you've reached the old age of eighty or more,
There are many odd things you'd love to ignore.

A Kick at Old Age
Aiming a foot at a dangling sock, he cursed:
'This bloody old age thing gets bloody well worse!'

Last Apples
Like the last apples attached to a bough,
We hang on as long as time will allow.

Leftover Time
The leftover years, when mating is through,
Provide us with time, old hopes to pursue.

Longevity's Token
There's nothing can beat, with old age so hard,
Receiving the Queen's monarchical card.

Luck
How lucky we are if our living ends first:
The symptoms of ageing can only get worse.

Middle Age
It seems middle age is akin to a hill:
We see the way up as a test of one's will.

Mind and Matter
Age is a case of mind over matter;
If you don't mind, things aren't going to matter.

Mobility
Mobility lessens as years fly by;
The lesson is don't stop having a try.

Muscles
Old timers should know that it's of the essence
Their over-stretched muscles obtain convalescence.

Mutual Support
The best of advice old age ever taught
Was giving each other mutual support.

New Pleasure
Smiling at babies peeping from cover
Brings great pleasure, as oldies discover.

No Letting Go
Our retirement days are all consumed
By unexpected roles we've assumed.

Octogenarian
Now he's completed his eightieth span,
He thinks he's become an intelligent man.

Old Age
When virile days have disappeared
Hard lives must thrive on soft settees.

Old Sages
Given the number of things they've been told,
Intelligence ought to favour the old.

Patient Waiting
The shorter our term that's still remaining,
The longer we keep our patience waiting.

Penchants
The average man has a penchant for pleasure;
Retired, he fancies a pension forever.

Pleasures
Seeking pleasures today, while vigour's at hand,
We tend to ignore what our dotage has planned.

Pleasures of Life
Pleasures of life are there to be tasted;
Time is measured, don't let them be wasted.

The Previous Stage
You cannot evade the pangs of old age,
So make a feast of the previous stage.

Recuperation
Our years in vigorous occupation
Deserve some later recuperation.

Regeneration
Gladly I find it's lately become
Son and father from father and son.

Reminiscences
Reminiscences, frequently told,
Don't endear the young to the old.

Retirement
Retirement, why bruit I your praises?
I haven't slaved this hard in ages!

Retiring
Likes cats that curl up in front of the fire,
We finish our jobs and snugly retire.

Shakespeare
Keeping Shakespeare to read when retired
Assumes by then you won't have expired.

Simple Things
The delight we find in simple things
Is recompense for what ageing brings.

Slowing Down
Once known as the ultimate man of action,
He found relaxing his latter attraction.

Snoozing
When you've turned eighty you'll notice quite soon
That you take a snooze in the afternoon.

Spills and Pills
It's tough when we're told to be mopping our spills,
And we loathe being told to take those darned pills.

That Certain Age
Many roles are played on the marital stage,
Some unfittingly tried at that certain age.

TLC
When old couples walk arm in arm,
What they share is a caring calm.

Trials of Life
It's no surprise generations differ:
Life's trials become increasingly stiffer.

Unretirement
The aim when that gainful span has expired
Is keeping one's faculties unretired.

Volte-face
Looking ahead, the young man yearns;
Old men suffer other concerns.

Vows of Spring
When old we cling to the vows of spring:
The promise of warmth the swallows bring.

Years
How women look gives age its meaning;
Men are as old as how they're feeling.

Young Again
I wished I was young, then heard the refrain:
'I don't want to go through all that again!'

CHAPTER 3 with 28 two-liners

AMBITION & JOBS

Achievement
Achievement depends on focused intent
Rejecting that villain, wilful dissent.

Aims
Achieving your aim in a piecemeal way
Assumes that your pep won't fritter away.

Ambition
Our every kind of want and need
Demands we on ambition feed.

Ambitions
Nursing ambitions for this thing or that,
You'll need the patience of Thomas the cat.

Ancestral Ambition
Of all the ambitions we put to the test,
Becoming an ancestor's nature's behest.

Anti-climax
Rapid success in one's early career
Makes anti-climax a prospect to fear.

Application
To follow a genius needs concentration:
The train of thought mustn't miss the odd station.

Apprenticeship
The apprentice can't practise his craft until
He's completely mastered the requisite skill.

Chaps
The sort of chap who hitches his breeches
Will never prefer cms to inches.

Clutter
No job is complete and deserving of pay
Until all the clutter's been ushered away.

Competence and Contentment
Manual skills where one's competence lies
Provide contentment on which the mind thrives.

Congratulation
Whenever according congratulation,
We're tacitly showing our admiration.

Creativity
If what you want is to be creative,
Don't let your ego become deflated.

Designers
Of all professions, designers have it:
The power to dictate our latest habit.

Desire
A strong desire is what we need
To make our enterprise succeed.

Extended Success
Success demands unrelenting endeavour;
We shouldn't expect it to last forever.

Hopeful Perfection
Seeking perfection's a hopeful intention
Requiring a lengthy implementation.

Ideas
Exchanging ideas can make for success;
Assess, however, who's coming off best.

Influence
It's terribly simple sourcing a job
When either mummy or daddy's a nob.

Inventing
Inventors know what inventing takes
By learning from their many mistakes.

Jobbers
Two workmen arrived, the boss and his mate,
And I was amazed that neither was late.

Lady Professors
In earlier times most professors were male,
Now erudite ladies seem set to prevail.

Motivation
Admitting a lapse, in his own estimation,
He's clearly in need of some fresh motivation.

Photo Fortune
On wedding day with the bride all a flutter,
He makes a fortune from clicking his shutter.

Skill
Skill's an ingredient of manifold tasks.
Without it the novice aimlessly grafts.

Small Letters
Young graphic designers use very small letters;
We'd like to decode them, but eyesight won't let us.

Specialist
Through concentration a specialist brings
The keenest of skills to recondite things.

Worthy Pride
Pride in one's work is a worthy intention,
As is obtaining the price of perfection.

CHAPTER 4 with 14 two-liners

APPEARANCE

Beauty
Perceptions of beauty are not universal;
Forever they're sure to remain controversial.

Beauty and Use
Objects deemed to be truly beautiful
Seldom prove to be equally useful.

Becoming
Donkeys consider refusal becoming:
Better look handsome than brimful of running!

Beguiling Smile
Unlike the wry smirk, a delightful smile
Is doubtless aware of how to beguile.

Catwalks
Catwalks compete, but when all's said and done
Even the dawdler one really can't shun.

Fashion
The fate of whatever today's the passion
Is ever hereafter seeming old-fashioned.

Fashion Passion
Scouring her mind for spectacular robes,
The fashion designer frantically probes.

Glamour
Beauty prevails in natural ways:
Glamour relies on lotions and sprays.

Glamour Queen
While her natural assets had their allure,
She'd apply some disguise, just to make sure.

Impressing
To impress, we trust to sartorial measures;
A peacock has only to shiver its feathers.

Impressions
Each person leaves a private impression;
Some briefly made deserve a concession.

Ostentation
Smoking Cuban cigars in lieu of cheroots,
He spoke like a stooge too big for his boots.

Show-offs
When ladies go dining to show off their rings,
They're mainly the choicest of granny's old things.

Wrinkles
Facial wrinkle-lines show our nature,
Politely claims the portrait painter.

CHAPTER 5 with 28 two-liners

ART

Abstract
Abstract art performs a subtle transition
Conceived in the mind, transformed as depiction.

Appreciation
Rather a gallery housing great works
Than houses with copies of minimal worth.

Art
The source of art is imagination;
What we see is its manifestation.

Art and Nature
The artist, intrigued by nature's attraction,
Never succeeds in attempted enhancement.

Art Critiques
Art historians interpret old pictures,
Artists distantly cursing their scriptures.

Art Exhibitions
Some consider the art a distraction,
Finding old frames a greater attraction.

Art Worth
Appreciation of artists' work
Carries a hint of increasing worth.

Artful Art
His painting ranged from a smooth-back iguana
To a penguin's square egg and a straight banana.

Artists
From what lies before them, the artists derive
Perspectives on life that enlighten our eyes.

Arts
Art bestows its own label on others:
Music, poetry, fathers and mothers.

Bad Dabs
No artist can alter their watercolours:
Additional dabs won't blend with the others.

Conjectural Art
Conjectural art that shocks us today
Is trite ephemera, doomed to decay.

Culture
A great mosaic of multiple parts,
Culture embraces all of the arts.

Homage to Objects
Disregarding every facsimile made,
The ardent still flock where the object's displayed.

Impressionism
The impressionist's art is succinctly defined
As an ism that left its impression behind.

Lens and Easel
The role of a camera's mostly recording,
Freeing the artist to follow his calling.

Mallet and Palette
Sculptors chip marble with chisel and mallet,
Like painters who always stick to one palette.

Nature and Art
No matter how great the artist's intensity,
Art cannot penetrate nature's complexity.

Objects of Art
Most objects of art created by man
Tend to live longer than any man can.

Optional Wealth
They who see wealth in every old picture
Need to peruse an earlier scripture.

Painting
Learning how to paint's a sort of obsession
That leaves behind a lasting impression.

Picture
A picture can capture a blink in time:
And yet can linger in memory's mind.

Pictures
Stately houses display their dukes and sirs;
A view or two's what the bourgeois prefers.

Portrayals
As actors portray their parts in a play,
The artist depicts them in his own way.

Sculpting
Some sculptors will only chip what they feel,
While others insist on cloning what's real.

Sketch
It doesn't need much to remember a scene;
The merest of sketches is all that you need.

Sketch Exhibition
When perusing hung images sketch by sketch,
It's amazing to see what some of them fetch.

Triple Dimensions
Paintings that triple dimensions can capture
Merit the praise of the critical sculptor.

CHAPTER 6 with 148 two-liners

BEHAVIOUR

Acknowledgement
No matter how slight their notion appears,
Always acknowledge another's ideas.

Absence
When an absence requires an explanation,
The answer's a lie or justification.

Absurdity
The end of something completely absurd
Occurs when laughs of derision are heard.

Action
Follow the lead of the first of the few:
Always take action when action is due.

Aloofness
In essence, aloofness looks distant and cool,
Which somehow can make one appear like a fool.

Arrogance
Arrogant people don't get very far:
They're too busy telling us who they are.

Assertions
Yes, check if the other's assertion is right,
But note! One dog's bark is another dog's bite.

Audition
On arriving there our stress-signs compare:
A flick of the hair, a fidget elsewhere.

Awkward
Loath to accept either even or odd,
He clearly belonged to the awkward squad.

The Bad and the Good
The good among us need to combine,
In order to keep the bad in line.

Being Ignored
Bearing characteristics in common accord,
Politicians and actors hate being ignored.

Benefit Louts
Let's banish those louts with malicious intents,
Whose benefits come at some others' expense.

Besting Others
There's an urge to best others some can't contain,
No matter how trivial their ultimate gain.

Bitching
No matter how all the bitching began,
It certainly ain't no place for a man.

Bravado
Bravado's a show, disguised as valour,
Avoiding the cries of battle's clamour.

Broken Promise
Akin to a bubble, suddenly burst,
A promise dishonoured can't be reversed.

Certitude
An unrelenting certitude
Reflects a stubborn attitude.

Change of Mind
It doesn't show weakness to change one's mind;
Strength's often required to be so inclined.

Charm
Charm's not a veneer, an applied cosmetic,
Rather a quality, subtly magnetic.

Charm and Flattery
Kin to charm in its artful intention,
Flattery practises sly deception.

Cliques
No cloistered cliques who deem themselves scholarly
Suffer voices from wider society.

Cocksure
Arrogance attaches to someone cocksure:
The sort of assumption it's hard to endure.

Communication
When rivals can't come to a resolution
Communication is half the solution.

Complacency
Complacency lacks the makings of fame;
Self-satisfaction is all it can claim.

Complainers
The visitor dusting a picture frame's
The sort of person who loves to complain.

Compromising
Of course there are times when we compromise,
Most notably when supplies don't arrive.

Confidence
Confidence always engenders respect;
The wonders it works ensure that effect.

Consideration
Those who exhibit consideration
Merit a nod of appreciation.

Contentment
Contentment's a treasure you need to guard.
And best disguised when you grumble and carp.

Conviviality
Conviviality's worn as a mask
While negotiators warm to their task.

Courteous Conversion
Mock politeness employed persistently
Might convert to genuine courtesy.

Creating Impressions
Always wearing a pleasant expression
Tends to create a fetching impression.

Cursing
Our living encompasses cursing and lying;
Some cursing is useful, there's no denying.

Cynical Comments
Cynical comments expressed with insistence
Are desperate attempts to cover up ignorance.

Cynicism
While cynical manners approach the uncouth,
Cynics adhere to their version of truth.

Deceiver
A slicker with manners polite and disarming
Might dissemble a hustler, vilely alarming.

Decisions
In general we stick by decisions we've taken;
However, like waves, they admit variation.

Decorum
Decorum expects good taste and propriety:
In common neglect by today's society.

Defensive Laughter
Laughter is sometimes a form of defence,
Until the aggressor spots the pretence.

Derision
Laughing at others is way out of line:
Scorn and derision can poison the mind.

Disagreement
Disagreement allows for opposite views,
Provided no untoward action ensues.

Discussion
Discussion is mostly more calm than debate
Unless in the former things start to inflate.

Earful
When some rowdy louts began to look fearful,
He was content just to give them an earful.

Effort
Begrudging effort when required
Is not the way to be inspired.

Emulation
Emulation may help you succeed;
Imitation's the way to proceed.

Endeavours
With fruitless endeavours you'll have to contend
That apple you're watching will drop in the end.

Error
He who never admits to an error
Probably lies or lacks in endeavour.

Excusings
Excusings we use engagingly vary
From absolute truth to the tale of a fairy.

Eye Rolling
When people are said to be rolling their eyes,
What they're really thinking is hard to surmise.

Eye to Eye
When someone's not looking you straight in the face,
It may be from shyness or patent disgrace.

Failings
Where we damn another's deed,
We may not ourselves succeed.

Faint-hearted
After promising moments kept passing him by,
He regretted he'd not had the courage to try.

Fingers
Fingers tight-clenched have alternative plans
To pleading peace by the shaking of hands.

Forbearance
The self-control forbearance requires
Finds its limit when patience expires.

Fresh Acquaintance
A fresh acquaintance we tend to believe,
Unless there's some later slip we perceive.

Furtiveness
Furtive behaviour raises suspicion,
Causing concern of a rogue's volition.

Good Breeding
Since manners began, two signs of good breeding
Have been one's ways of drinking and feeding.

Gratitude's Progress
Gratitude's not only a juvenile trait:
'Please' can come quite early, 'thanks' terribly late.

Guest
Grabbing the most from your host's hospitality
Smacks of a hotel customer's mentality.

Gullibility
The truly gullible can't realize
That lies are really not truths in disguise.

Hate
Hate is a stain that's hard to erase,
Though patience sustained in time repays.

Her Mission
The woman who rants when you'd like her to listen
Is doubtless absorbed in her personal mission.

Hesitation
Exaggeration of hesitation
Can reach the stage of procrastination.

Honest Denial
Those three words 'To be honest', one can't deny,
Are as likely as not to preface a lie.

Humiliation
While stitching the wound of humiliation,
Try to encrypt your identification.

Hypocrisy
Perpetration of blatant hypocrisy
Serves the same aim as wilful dishonesty.

Hypocrite
The hypocrite always must stay alert,
Or else his pretensions never will work.

Hypocritical Risk
Hypocrisy's a risky endeavour
When focused on an intimate pleasure.

Hypocritical Wit
Hypocrisy sometimes outwits
The innocent targets it hits.

Idleness
The source of idleness might be sought
In minds deprived of critical thought.

Idlers
Like pampered cats they thrive on sleep:
Though toiling not, the idlers reap.

Idling
Some idling counts as honest relief
From arduous toil where time's a thief.

Indecency
Indecency shares, with scant disparity,
All the main traits of blatant vulgarity.

Indignation
Those who're annoyed and display indignation
May also suffer acute irritation.

Indiscretion
An occasional act of indiscretion
Can give to others a dreadful impression.

Inquisitive People
Inquisitive people think they're unique,
While those around them are peeved by their cheek.

Inquisitiveness
Inquisitive people are strong on persistence;
Their weakness is never to mind their own business.

Instincts
An instinct triggers impulsive behaviour:
Experience tempers it in our favour.

Invitation
A note declining an invitation
Might include a convenient invention.

Irascibility
His manner is gross when he's most irate;
I rate it's his least acceptable trait.

Lapses
How well we fight for our way of living,
Yet lapse at times in being forgiving.

Lazing
The slothful can stay sufficiently lazy
Only by being efficiency-crazy.

Lies
To be lied about earns no one a prize:
Reproof applies to those telling the lies.

Lies and Truths
Lies reach by express their destination,
While truths are tested at every station.

Loafers
The loafer droops like a burnt-out rocket
And tends to stand with his hands in his pockets.

Loudspeaker
Though not a mandate, it's often the way
That loudest voices have least to convey.

Lying
If through some circumstance one's found to have lied,
What can't be denied is the loss of one's pride.

Manners
Good manners abound in polite society;
Good lookers find them a lesser necessity.

Misdemeanours
Sinning in secret the miscreant can handle;
Misdemeanours in public will cause a scandal.

Morons
When morons encounter the odd or strange,
They snigger and jeer as if they're deranged.

Muddy Water
When everything's shipshape and neatly in order,
Some nitwit will leap in and muddy the water.

Mutual Trust
A party reneging on mutual trust
Deceives another and leaves them nonplussed.

Naughtiness
A measure of naughtiness might be excused,
Provided, of course, that it isn't abused.

New Leaf
The new leaf that someone said they'd turned over
Was probably one from a four-leaf clover.

No Problem
For people who deem themselves fully adept,
Impossible isn't a word they'd accept.

Obstinacy
Most obstinate people won't yield to conversion:
They're either admired or engender aversion.

Obtuseness
Irritation rises when someone's obtuse,
Especially when there's no obvious excuse.

Odd Comment
To believe a comment you've just overheard
Is unrealistic and frankly absurd.

Odd Obligations
Some obligations are self-imposed
Without us recalling how they arose.

On Greeting
Though someone you greet is finely attired,
For deference further cause is required.

Ostentatious Behaviour
Ostentation's a plague on the face of the earth,
But affords the unwealthy some cynical mirth.

People
Break any habit you once might have had
Of rating people all good or all bad.

Perseverance
However severe the opposition,
Perseverance will strengthen your mission.

Persuasion
Amenable people, too easily led,
Aren't able to notice persuasion ahead.

Pessimists
Like metal detectorists scanning a field,
The pessimist never expects a great yield.

Pests
So many people turn out to be pests,
We wonder if we're as bad as the rest.

Pleasantest Vice
Among the temptations that daily entice,
The hardest to shun is one's pleasantest vice.

Pleasantry
A pleasantry shows one can be polite,
At least when the other man's still in sight.

Politely Bored
To listen politely when frightfully bored,
Is slightly preferred to being ignored.

Politeness
Excessive politeness tends to suggest
The person you've met is out to impress.

Pride
Pride is all right when you keep it inside:
It's letting it out that people deride.

Pride and Satisfaction
Satisfaction is pleased but quiet:
Rowdy pride can incite a riot!

Pubbing
Where Friday night pubbing can lead to a brawl,
You need to be keeping away from it all.

Qualities
Honesty, probity, total fidelity
Cluster, conveying a sense of integrity.

Quizzicality
Quizzical looks are a way of conveying
What's in one's mind, without openly saying.

Reconciliation
Reconciliation rewards endeavour
In bringing quarrelsome parties together.

Reliability
A person's pious reliability
Will likely hike their desirability.

Renegades
Whoever as an expert masquerades
Must risk the ranks of unmasked renegades.

Reputations
Reputations derive from common belief;
The loss of one comes as a welcome relief.

Responsible
A responsible person takes great care
Few errors occur beyond their repair.

Richards
Those christened Richard soon after their birth
May later be plagued by outbursts of mirth.

Righting Wrongs
Attempting to right all the wrongs you encounter
Could lead to unwonted mental disaster.

Roguery
Rogues who have chosen the wrong direction
Shouldn't resent some useful correction.

Rubbish
In parts of some towns the ruffians' appeal is
Chucking their rubbish in other blokes' wheelies.

Scandal
Those who recycle a scandal for bother
Are probably worse than the story's author.

Scouts
Their Chief would wager that very few Scouts
Would gain the status of fully fledged louts.

Self-justification
Self-justification takes the place
Of self-improvement, to man's disgrace.

Serving no Purpose
A storm in a teacup isn't worth drinking:
No more than baling a ship that's sinking.

Sham
It's said that manners maketh man;
Their semblance, though, might cloak a sham.

Shameful Defence
When people do things that lead to their shame,
Their defence is to call on duty to blame.

Sin
With no restraint over inclination,
Sin persists in its implementation.

Sinners
While we reprove those we know to have sinned,
The sins we can't prove we have to rescind.

Skiving
He who in skiving chooses to revel
Risks his soul in the noose of the Devil.

Slackers
Slackers discover which rules are the loosest,
And save on graft with the meanest excuses.

Slander
A slanderous statement made by a liar
Generates rumour like smoke from a fire.

Spite
Sensing the germination of spite,
Remove the root and cast it from sight.

Strictures
Where a pupil is picked as a prime example,
The strictures they've set must be helpful and ample.

Swanks
Alas, there are swanks who think they're appealing
And try to sound clever beyond believing.

Swearing
With those who keep swearing you'll probably find
F is the letter that first comes to mind.

Sybarite
A sybarite reaches heights of delight,
Keeping his vagaries clear out of sight.

Telegenic
Today, the way to be telegenic
Is looking not cool but energetic.

Telltales
We don't associate gossip with males;
They have no truck with those give away tales.

Trusty Memory
Though we don't associate lying with trust,
For the liar a trusty memory's a must.

Vagrancy
Evading tax and domestic matters,
The vagrant degrades to rags and tatters.

Verbal Indigestion
When indecent suggestions are hard to swallow,
Verbal indigestion is likely to follow.

Wastrels
They cheat their lives who take, not give,
And working at not working live.

Winners
Don't envy those who are openly winners;
We each have our share of greatness within us.

Worth
Since no alternative measurement can,
Behaviour defines the worth of a man.

CHAPTER 7 with 56 two-liners

BUSINESS

Agents
Agents provide a percentage service,
Taking a tithe from their clients' purses.

Apart From Together
Assembling specialists brings them together:
It sets them apart from the rest, however.

Assignments
If you complete your assignments today,
You'll welcome the start of a fresh new day.

Automatic
So many actions are now automatic
They're taking the place of what we call magic.

Backhanders
Backhanders frequently ease big deals;
Illegal dealings a frontman conceals.

Captains of Industry
Captains of industry haven't got teams,
They borrow the term to win our esteem.

Carbon Copy
A carbon copy is sensibly meant
As confirmation of what has been sent.

Changing Times
From eight hours five to twenty-four seven!
Those torrid old times now seem like heaven.

Charity Shops
Charity shops could last throughout time
Now that some happily trade online.

Clincher
Clinching a deal, with a wry little smile,
Reveals the deployment of winsome guile.

Clock Watching
Once, watching the time brought typists disgrace:
Now, using a screen, the clock's in their face.

Committees
A committee of one makes rapid decisions;
A quorum of more wreaks fraught inhibitions.

Compliance
One tenth of the day pertains to one's job,
And ninety percent compliance-forms rob.

Confidential
Some products have to remain confidential,
Especially when they're experimental.

Confusing to Use
An aspect that makes some products inferior
Is failure to make their user guides clearer.

Connoisseurs
The spirit that motivates entrepreneurs
Requires the control of well versed connoisseurs.

Consumer Concerns
When firms have rules for accepting returns,
They're prone to promote consumer concerns.

Contacts Count
Publishers flung their rejections at her.
Contents don't rate: it's contacts that matter.

Decision Making
Most company heads make rapid decisions,
Frequently leading to staffing excisions.

Economics
While the study of wealth is about investing:
Economics itself is often depressing.

Effusive Greeting
No prolonged and effusive greeting
Guarantees a productive meeting.

Executive Constraints
Those skilful attainments one daily provides
Are later constrained by executive ties.

Falling Through
While dealings that fail are said to fall through,
Schemes that fall short one oughtn't pursue.

Freelance
To ensure his work was researched and timely,
He purchased a house next door to a library.

Futility
Futility reigns when strategic discussions
Resolve into monologues, thwarting decisions.

Generic
If similar products can't show they're specific,
They will have to agree to being generic.

Glossy Paper
Printers of forms-to-fill need to rethink
Their glossy paper which baffles dry ink.

Half Time
'Give me half a minute' receptionists say
As you clutch the receiver half of the day.

Head over Heart
The young executive, dressed for the part,
Trusts to his head to temper his heart.

Incompetence
In hierarchical firms executives rise
Until their incompetence can't be denied.

Incumbency
A new incumbent, appointed on promise,
Mightn't achieve the prestige of his office.

Inhibition
His projects all failed when indecision
Became a prelude to inhibition.

Lousing Up
The architect's plan for a house, with luck
Will find a builder who won't louse it up.

Mail Order
Half of our gadgets are born overseas:
With home-grown products we're more at ease.

Networking
Networking starts with the making of contacts,
Aiming in time for the signing of contracts.

Noxious Merchandise
What worth do they set on human lives
Who fail to mark noxious merchandise?

Obsolescence
Where products are based on planned obsolescence,
Quality's probably not of the essence.

Offers
Attractive though two-for-one offers might be,
In the business of shopping nothing's for free.

On the Level
A deal on the level that's clearly defined
Ought not to accede to being declined.

Paper Game
Filing all the papers one ought to retain
Of late has become a preposterous game.

Percentages
Full fifty percent's a bargain offer:
It's the 'Up to' that causes the bother!

Quality Wares
They ask us to purchase their quality wares
Then we've to return them for needed repairs.

Recruitment
In recruiting, a useful asset to have
Is the knack of sorting the wheat from the chaff.

Regulations
Rigid restrictions and regulations
Inhibit trading between the nations.

Restrictions
Rules and strictures imposed on us
Cramp the genie in genius.

Results
Decisions made are based on prediction;
Results are our judgements' vindication.

Robots
Most firms assessing production-line beavers
Find robots outpace their greatest achievers.

Seamy Side
Where greed overrides a patriot's pride,
Commercial life shows its seamier side.

Service
Long service once brought you a tankard or watch;
Today's might just manage a snifter of scotch.

Signs of the Times
You know the makers are under the hammer
When ink costs more than their printer-cum-scanner.

The Small Print
All the small print your vendor supplies
Beats cloaking a clown in cryptic disguise.

Teamwork
Individuals tread their own ways:
Teamwork requires that nobody strays.

Times of Change
In times of change it's unlikely to follow
That father and son will plough the same furrow.

Trade Cards
There are crowds of trade cards I've pinned on a board
That I have to admit are mostly ignored.

Unsureness
In critical meetings, as many have found,
It's best not to speak when unsure of one's ground.

Yours or Theirs?
Like big stores and banks and the BBC,
The Government says it's for you and me.

CHAPTER 8 with 18 two-liners

CELEBRITY & FAME

Appraising Praise
Valuing praise is a delicate matter:
It depends on the worth of those flatter.

Celebrity Ranking
Whatever their rank in celebrity,
They're fed with jobs by the powers that be.

Celebrity Wreckage
Peering back through the edge of posterity,
The scene is England, wrecked by celebrity.

Celebrity's Gist
If you've missed the gist of instant celebrity,
It's simply those with a known physiognomy.

Clippings
Now the prestige of celebrity's slipping,
They make new programmes assembling old clippings.

Dodging Fame
Oh, not to be famous and playing the game
Of dodging the press, and just living again!

Egos
When those with charisma suffer a fall,
The bigger their ego the lower they crawl.

Excessive Celebrities
Celebrities come, as all of us know;
But, try as we might, we can't make them go.

Fame and Praise
Fame is imposed just for being well known;
Praise is bestowed when due cause has been shown.

Fame's Attraction
Fame is a motor of potent attraction:
An engine engendering lust and passion.

Feeling Good
When tactile hinting at praise abounds,
Flattery feels as good as it sounds.

Little Chance
Opportunity's unlikely to knock
Unless you're on telly around the clock.

Pomposity
Taking celebrity then pomposity,
Try to discover the least disparity!

Popularity
Popularity walked a step behind glory;
Now it's absorbed by invasive celebrity.

Sad Celebs
Ageing celebs end as sad retirers,
Selling their wrinkles to advertisers.

Soap Star
As soon as a soap star speaks her first line,
Her income increases beyond the sublime.

Telebrity
Embraced by celebrity's wider reach,
Telebrities populate TV's niche.

Wealth
Most punters resent celebrities' wealth,
Deriding 'earnings' when 'plunder' is meant.

CHAPTER 9 with 77 two-liners

CONCEPTS

Achievement
Achievement depends on focused intent
Rejecting that villain, wilful dissent.

Actuality
Actuality tells us you really are you;
Without it we'd certainly be in the stew.

Anticipation's Dilemma
Anticipation's a wretched dilemma;
It keeps you waiting for ever and ever.

Banality
Banality plumbs unoriginal minds;
Frivolity follows, a trifle behind.

Blatant Temptation
Where blatant temptation displays its wares,
It tests desire as to whether it dares.

Botheration
Resentment is brother to indignation,
As brother-in-law is to botheration.

Coincidence
Coincidence can't predict what arises:
Its only resort is the law of surprises.

Complexity
Complexity challenges understanding;
Simplicity's questions are less demanding.

Compromise
When indecision can't get off the fence,
Compromise offers a halfway pretence.

Consistency
Consistency's interest is staying the same:
Insisting on singing a single refrain.

Constancy
Constancy wears a ring on its finger,
Trusting its band for ever will linger.

Consumerism
Consumerism presumes addiction,
And envy adds its own contribution.

Counting the Hours
Without direction or goal that inspires,
Effort degrades to the counting of hours.

Courage
Courage and valour lie dormant inside us
Till grief or danger, unwonted, arises.

Curiosity
Curiosity's able to generate fear,
Though it's prone to retreat if real perils appear.

Currying Praise
When people seek comment on what they achieve,
It's done for the praise they might also receive.

Deception
Folly will always enjoy being told
It looks so young when it's growing so old.

Differing
While differing concepts are hard to restrain,
The notion of changing remains just the same.

Disappointment
In case our hopes should go awry,
Disappointment is standing by.

Discretion's Decision
Discretion's a choice that we need to take
But sometimes leads to an awful mistake.

Distinctions
Discretion is prudence and carefulness linked;
Its cousin discreteness keeps items distinct.

Downs and Ups
While slacking abides with the lower legions,
Enterprise rises to still higher regions.

Downstream
Only a river can flow downstream
To tell the tale of where it has been.

Envy
Resenting another's prized possession,
Envy's a product of admiration.

Excellence
Excellence only comes at a premium:
A step below sits the happy medium.

Extravagance
Extravagance mainly reveals its face
When overindulgence is taking place.

Face
Innocence looks you straight in the face:
Guiltiness turns away in disgrace.

Feasibility
Feasibility tells us what we can manage
From something quite simple to fixing a marriage.

Fickleness
Fickleness wanders away without pause,
Causing us grief it repeats with remorse.

Flattery
Glib words of praise can raise expectations;
Flattery publishes false perceptions.

Flexibility
Flexibility lets things bend without breaking,
The need for which hinges on what one is making.

Folly and Wisdom
Folly encourages swift intervention:
Wisdom advises some prior reflexion.

Fortuity's Reliance
Fortuity doesn't rely on a thing:
It just waits to see what the future might bring.

Give and Take
Be it giving and taking or tit for tat,
Reciprocity has a response off pat.

Grieving
Loss ineluctably leads to grief:
Grieving pursues the route to relief.

Hesitating
'I'm glad that I did,' and 'I wish that I had.'
Hesitation's traits are as good as they're bad.

Honest Denial
The words 'To be honest', one cannot deny,
Are as likely as not to preface a lie.

Humility
By way of avoiding a public disgrace,
Humility tries to keep pride in its place.

Ignorance
Ignorance plays the part of a fool,
But wisdom ignores him - as a rule.

Impartiality
Impartiality's hale and hearty
Until a backhander joins the party.

Implausibility
Glibness endorses implausibility;
Rigorous thought enforces integrity.

In Contrast
Frivolity's attitude's devil-may-care;
Philosophy wears a more serious air.

Indulgence
Indulgence smacks of unlimited pleasure
And lacks for rigour in similar measure.

Ineptitude
As experience grows with the passage of time,
Ineptitude measures a steady decline.

Initiative
Denying failure's continuous threat,
Initiative claims to forge right ahead.

Knowing
Ignorance ranges the scale of being:
Knowledge reaches as far as forgetting.

Lying and Honesty
While lying feeds on guilt and deception,
Honesty deals in exoneration.

Malice
Justice flows like limpid water:
Malice shows through turbid matter.

Mediation
Appreciation is mediation
Between acceptance and consummation.

Modesty
Modesty isn't the kinsman of pride:
Under a bushel its talents reside.

Modesty's Followers
Modesty follows the course of action
People feel holds the strongest attraction.

More Probable
If an unlikelihood cannot decide,
Something more probable ought to be tried.

Passion
Possessed of emotions overwhelming,
Passion surpasses our understanding.

Persuasive Deception
Plausibility thrives on deception
And smart persuasion, veiled from detection.

Plausibility
Plausibility dallies with truth
Often enough to warrant reproof.

Practice
If practice proceeds in the right direction
It's bound to achieve the aim of perfection.

Praise
Countering claims of over-temerity,
Praise is weighed on the scales of sincerity.

Probability
Probability smiles at possibility,
Knowing it's closer to actuality.

Resentment's State
If resentment creates an envious state,
Say *they* have the icing but *you* have the cake.

Retrogression
When retrogression changes its mind,
It's pleased to leave its history behind.

Shy and Polite
Shadows appear to be shy and polite,
Always refraining from taking the light.

Sincerity
Sincerity never stoops to deception
But chooses truth without any exception.

Sleep
Sleep is a stranger who works in the night
On notions ranging from wrath to delight.

Solitude
Solitude has no cause to be lonely,
Recalling times beknown to it only.

Sophistry
To deceive or simply to draw attention,
Sophistry uses false argumentation.

Subconsciousness
At times the subconscious can lead us astray
Without us knowing the games it can play.

Success and Failure
Success in its prime seems all-prevailing,
But even success succeeds in failing.

Superiority
Superiority endorses a scheme
Where others are held in lower esteem.

Superstition
The influence of superstition
Hatches many an inhibition.

Symmetry
To balance out classical approbation,
Symmetry has to accept disaffection.

Tact
Tact has a subtle, sensitive touch:
All it requires to achieve so much.

Veneration
Veneration borrows from old mythology,
Adding new virtues and tokens of chivalry.

Veracity
Memory paints delightful pictures:
Truth arises from sterner strictures.

Virtue
When virtue has cause to prove its own case,
Its image suffers in saving its face.

Vocal Support
While wishful thinking is speaking the truth,
Necessity adds some words of excuse.

Ways Ahead
'Incremental' advances with regular strides;
'Incidental' on risky hitch-hiking relies.

Wisdom and Folly
Wisdom's domain has a limited range:
Folly's extent permits infinite reins.

CHAPTER 10 with 36 two-liners

EDUCATION

Best Remembered
Not forgetting the basics that school days taught,
We remember best what experience bought.

Calculators
Hand calculators ought to be banned
Till mental maths is well in command.

Curricula
A school's curriculum vaguely applies
To the intellect of average guys.

Doubted Knowledge
If on occasion your knowledge is doubted,
Right then there's not much can be done about it.

Early Learning
Fortunate children learn by example,
Others in ways more experimental.

Educational Expectation
In family homes throughout the nation
Trust women to spread their education.

Elucidation
While teachers allude to elucidation,
Their pupils are happy with explanation.

Enough's Enough
Scholars who wear a cap and a gown
Don't need a solipsistical frown.

Exegesis
Expounding a critical exegesis
Sometimes amounts to creating a thesis.

Experiencing
Experience travels as far as it goes,
Amassing knowledge that constantly grows.

Fears for Careers
A narrow, illiberal education
Could limit a scholar's range of vocation.

Finals
University finals incur some concern
By implying that students have no more to learn.

Graduation
Hire her a gown, a cap and a hood:
Signs of learning she's not understood.

Head Pupil
As soon as a pupil's made head of his class,
He starts to wonder how long it will last.

Helpful Mistakes
Making mistakes can frequently prove
The simplest way to help you improve.

Hindsight
Of all the methods of learning known,
Hindsight retains a place of its own.

Itemizing
Items of knowledge we fail to learn
May one day be of major concern.

Knowledge
What passes for knowledge we've all been taught;
Accepted wisdom needs critical thought.

Learning
Learning embraces binuclear kinds:
Teaching of facts, education of minds.

Learning and Teaching
How do learning and teaching differ?
One's a receiver, one a giver.

Lecturers
Whenever lecturers say they'll be brief,
Everyone utters a sigh of relief.

Lecturing
To teach, one first had to learn how to stall;
To lecture, one needs to have learnt it all.

New Knowledge
Every new quantum of knowledge we gain
Adds further burdens to memory and brain.

Parents and Teachers
As meetings with teachers start to draw near,
Slight apprehension begins to appear.

Preparation
When waiting to face an examination
Much will depend on your prior preparation.

Selecting Reading
Ensuring people can read belongs to teaching;
Education tells them what's worthy of reading.

Spelling
Teaching your children how to spell
Sorely tests your patience as well.

Teach to Learn
Teach them the things to let them earn;
More than that, teach them how to learn!

Teacher
No matter how wise and how prudent,
Each teacher's forever a student.

Teacher and Taught
Teachers are people who've taught a doer,
And who, in their time, have each used a tutor.

Teachers and Pupils
Teachers itching to teach just might not have thought
That pupils don't share the same urge to be taught.

Textbook Clones
The textbook method of education
Churns out clones with a common dimension.

Teeth's Lesson
There's a good lesson all parents should teach:
Turn off the tap while you're brushing your teeth.

True Education
Education teaches us how to react.
The things we've all learnt are mere matters of fact.

Tutoring
Like talking in somebody else's sleep
Was how the tutor felt, earning his keep.

Versions of Learning
One can either learn by taking lessons
Or by asking people lots of questions.

CHAPTER 11 with 8 two-liners

ENVIRONMENT

Ecologists
Ecologists mooted a new profession
That showed our leaders a greener direction.

Farmers
They feed the soil with chemical dressings
That starve the land of natural blessings.

Food for Thought
Organics are overly priced in the store.
Foods tainted with chemicals ought to cost more.

The Gardener
So many creatures infest his displays,
He's tempted to stray to chemical sprays.

Green Planning
Green fingers alone can't rescue the planet:
We need a green plan, and us all to man it.

Green Talk
From constant talk of green behaviour
Allotment-holding reaps fresh favour.

Herbicides
Where herbicides kill agricultural weeds,
Wild birds are deprived of their edible seeds.

Insecticide
Insecticide and pesticide
Are other names for suicide.

CHAPTER 12 with 65 two-liners

EPITAPHS

Adventitious
As his theme was chance, it was quite propitious
He'd hit on the adjective adventitious.

Anon
Under his nostrils where bristles once grew,
He thundered abuse and his bluest jokes blew.

Artisanal Model
In many ways the artisanal model,
His habit was calling each task a doddle.

Beguiling Praise
His weakness was liking beguiling praise:
Succumbing to flattery seldom pays.

Bigwig
Those who deplored his behaviour at home
Never applauded when fanfares were blown.

Candour
Never a one to stray or philander,
He stayed on the route of truth and candour.

Claim to Fame
What spurred his writing was less acquisition:
More national honours through recognition.

Conceit
Such was the stature of his conceit,
Only his vanity could compete.

Critical Break
Sick of the critics, he took a long break.
Those who write nothing can't make a mistake.

Cure-all
His one panacea
Was taking to beer.

The Dame
Not one to sag after getting the sack,
Like a rubber ball she came bouncing back.

Dirty Old Man
Though detractors dubbed him a dirty old man,
It couldn't curtail the length of his span.

Encouragement
His way was disparagement:
His sort of encouragement.

Epitaphic Correctness
Folk write ahead to ensure their epitaph
Harbours no typo nor some different gaffe.

Expediency
Without becoming completely indecent,
His standards would lower when deemed expedient.

Exuberance
Constant exuberance fashioned his style;
His Merseyside accent stood out a mile.

Fame's Value
His fame didn't carry a value on it:
It couldn't be used to raise a deposit.

Famously Aged
He feared his celebrity
Bespoke his antiquity.

FEATURE CAMEO
*Try to detect the nine people below,
With only JP in the first person.*

For DT
While he'd worked in London he dreamt of Wales,
Constructing his verse and evocative tales.

For JB
A takeaway wasn't really his style:
The Ritz Hotel was the number he'd dial.

For FP
The bikes he made, so close to perfection,
Always promoted pride of possession.

For JP
I hear an echo of the words I pen:
That I was thoughtful of my fellow men.

For KD
He found life's comic element
His requisite ingredient.

For Lady D
As she entered the room all heads turned round,
Acknowledging what a kind person they'd found.

For MM
She swiftly proceeded from tatters to riches,
Revealing the value of vital statistics.

For NM
With strength of mind, shunning threats he incurred,
Still from his purpose he wasn't deterred.

For RB
Despite his tentative, modest beginnings,
Enterprise led to the mightiest winnings.

Frowning Brows
With frowning brows and some fore teeth missing,
He bore the looks of a listed building.

Hale and Hearty
With manners discreet she was hale and hearty,
And always dressed like a guest at a party.

Hedonism
Hedonism dictated his living,
His style of behaviour unforgiving.

Hero
He and his entourage traversed the crowd
Like the sun manoeuvres through drifting cloud.

His Life a Fluke
He always maintained that his life was a fluke;
One never heard medics receive his rebuke.

Idylls and Idols
While his idylls depicted pastoral scenes,
His idols created ethereal themes.

Imagination
His handicap was a poor education:
Imagination his rich compensation.

Insouciance
He tackled problems with placid insouciance,
Seeing solutions through limpid translucence.

Introspection
He always maintained that introspection
Made his life go in the right direction.

Lasciviousness
All her career, controversially dressed,
She'd never suppress her lasciviousness.

Legal Antidote
After big cases with ponderous reasoning,
His antidote was a little light reading.

Lingual Abuse
He used his tongue like a whetted blade:
With each abuse the keener it came.

List and Dispatch
When things needing doing harassed her mind,
She'd list and dispatch them one at a time.

Lord B
His life among ladies was deftly described:
A person to whom indiscretion applied.

Magic
While logic caused him an awful plight,
Magic must have taught him how to write.

Migrating Birds
Her depictions of birds migrating at dawn
Were as static as corsets, too tightly drawn.

Morals with Laurels
With the heart of a lion, kindness and morals,
A dependable fellow, he earned his laurels.

Noble Tradition
What he achieved, in his noble tradition,
Was reading speeches that others had written.

Normal
He'd joke being normal suited him well:
Halfway to heaven and halfway from hell.

Playing the Game
The way he played put others to shame;
His way, you see, was playing the game.

Poet and Stoic
In the grand alliance of poet and critic,
He never acknowledged which one was the stoic.

Poetic Contention
Throughout her days she voiced the contention
That versing was pleasure, not a profession.

Poetic Depth
A crystal fountain has hidden depths;
Her lucid poems were likewise blessed.

Poetic Fame
His poems, ostensibly misunderstood,
Occasioned more fame than they otherwise would.

Prejudice
A temperate, honest discerning person,
Prejudice reigned as his major aversion.

Purple and Blue
Although his regalia was purple all through,
It's said that his humour was bluer in hue.

Quality
Disdaining thought of boring equality,
His aim in life was fostering quality.

Reciprocation
His last consolation, when old and feeble,
Was being rude to objectionable people.

Restraint
He taught the young that a little restraint
Was how to avoid parental complaint.

Satiation
He'd frequently boast of feeling elated:
A state that booze, not good health, had created.

Shared Pride
Not one to admonish the pupils who tried,
He later was able to share in their pride.

Side Effect
Her later sculpting exuded emotion:
A side effect of the loving cup's potion.

Stooge
Smoking Cuban cigars in lieu of cheroots,
He spoke like a stooge, too big for his boots.

Timekeeper
His remit required him to clock in at eight,
And up to retirement he never came late.

Trainspotter
He claimed he preferred to wait on a station,
And cursed what he called 'that four-wheeled creation'.

The Underdog Man
To encourage beginners was always his plan;
At matches they called him the underdog man.

Unending Pleasure
While he wrote his work with unending pleasure,
He'd read it all at his chosen pleasure.

Unpretentious
He was a creature devoid of pretensions,
Providing few answers, rather more questions.

CHAPTER 13 with 126 two-liners

FAUNA & FLORA

Adder
Don't let an adder discover a spot
From which to uncoil and deploy its plot.

Animal Monikers
Jennies and fillies pinched the best names;
Vixens and bitches wish they could change.

Antics
Fine cracks between slabs are street-ants' retreats,
Odd bits from kebabs their transient treats.

April Song
Up in the willow trees warblers sing
As if to greet the awakening of spring.

April's Flowers
April's blossoming new-born flowers
With joy fill lovers' courting hours.

Bat
Finding food, a bat relies
On radar rather than eyes.

Beak-to-Beak
I've never watched birds cavort cheek-to-cheek:
The closest I've seen have been beak-to-beak.

Bee Line
Keep buzzing, young bee! Your prime endeavour
Is pleasing your idle queen forever.

Bird Preferences
Some birds prefer to flit on the wing:
Others have opted to sit and sing.

Birds
The rate at which Britain's small birds is falling
Is nothing less than truly appalling.

Birds' Needs
When you're putting out seeds on which the birds feed,
Remember it's also fresh water they need.

Birdsong
If you sit in springtime where trees belong,
The air comes alive with avian song.

Birdwatching
Elegant shelters surveying the sea
Watch terns and cormorants fishing for tea.

Black Paws
After blithely exhausting the great outdoors,
He'd lie down beside me, wet nose on black paws.

Blending Petals
Though bluebells and daffodils are separately seen,
They could ever so beautifully blend into green.

Brent Geese
Flocked in the harbour, backs spattered with hail,
Like knights in armour they challenge the gale.

Bull
In many respects, from rudder to prow,
A bull's akin to an udderless cow.

Canine Impatience
A pooch on its leash sits in restless impatience,
Its preference patently peregrinatious.

Canine Status
The popular theory is incorrect:
The dog is in thrall to one who's erect.

Cat Matters
On lampposts all over you'll spot, displayed,
Photos of cats that have recently strayed.

Cat Purr
Enwrapped in its fleece of softest fur,
A cat emits a contented purr.

Cat Threat
Cats in our gardens can impose that great threat
Of consequent outcomes we'd always regret.

Cats as Game
Now they've quit wearing their grouse shooting gear,
They're breeding kittens for bagging next year.

Choisya Selection
Which of the two of us picked the choisya?
I'm sure it was you who made the choice, dear.

Daffodil Time
Once your daffodil bulbs have been planted in rows,
You just patiently wait and hope each of them grows.

Deer
When foraging antlers come into sight,
The browse-line offers to measure their height.

Dewdrops
Not every dewdrop falls from a web:
Some of them quench the spider instead.

Dissembler
Beware the coiled adder basking in May;
Though seeming to sleep it's alert to prey.

Distraction
Among the ructions of jackdaws and rooks
Lie silent nestlings the hawk overlooks.

Dog Leavers
When people go out leaving dogs behind,
Our language becomes a tad less refined.

Doodle Dog
Design of that pooch, the francophile poodle,
Derived from strong hooch and infantile doodle.

Duckling
Lucky's the duckling that needs to seek cover,
It sneaks beneath its impervious mother.

Ducks and Drakes
To see that ducks don't make many mistakes,
There are different colours for ducks and drakes.

Electric Tail
Old fluffy-tail, seeking the acorns' location,
Recharges the garden's electrification.

Estimation
Animals aren't in the least way concerned
About reputations they've probably earned.

Expensive Trees
When trees are planted too close to fences
They're bound to lead to later expenses.

Exposure
A jet black crow in the crisp white snow
Doesn't quite know where it ought to go.

Extermination
Let us try not to exterminate
Our small busy friends who pollinate.

First Acquaintance
First meeting's a moment to smile and compare;
With dogs it's a rather more nosey affair.

Floral Deprivation
Blossoms in vases since who can tell when
Will never sense rain or sunshine again.

The Flower and the Worm
The sunken worm can't separate
The sounds that rain and beaks create!

Foreign Plants
Enwrap foreign plants in a frostproof shroud:
They're not with winter defences endowed.

Forsythia
Displaying bright petals before its green leaves,
The forsythia gives birth before it conceives.

Foxes
It's uncanny how foxes will stop and stare
As if to enquire if you really are there.

Fruity Friends
A multicultural affair
Are mango, fig and juicy pear.

Fussy Pussy
I watched a black pussy ascending a tree
And knew what it wanted, between you and me.

Garbage Flies
When residual garbage is left behind,
The presence of flies is easy to find.

Gardens in Flower
Gardens in flower our senses beguile:
Their scents and colours remind us to smile.

Glow-worms
Due to their nightly incandescence,
Glow-worms betray an eerie presence.

Good Bites
He cast by the weir where the gnats were in flight.
He'd gone there because he'd been promised good bites.

Grappling Blackbirds
You know your garden is great to inhabit
When rival blackbirds will grapple to grab it.

Green Woodpecker
Welcome green woodpecker greeting the dawn!
Keep probing for ants, aerating the lawn.

Gulls
Gulls scavenge their food on the rubbish tip:
A daily allowance in just one trip.

Happy Farrier
Happy the farrier whose pleasure's complete
When giving his customers' feet a treat.

The Horse
We have to consider the horse to be
The noblest creature in history.

House-fly
The house-fly used to be a pest:
It's buzz would never let us rest.

Kingfisher
All of a sudden a kingfisher flies,
Plumed to perfection, the sky its disguise.

Kittens
Kittens arrive having tightly closed eyes;
When they come open the world's a surprise.

Latin
Once, Latin was taken as proof of a scholar;
Now, it mainly gives names to fauna and flora.

Mammalian Locomotion
Primates rely on two arms or two legs;
The quadruped's favoured in this respect.

Matchmaker
The matchmaker spaces her snapdragons out,
With hopes for additional colours, no doubt.

Meddling
The bee that stings a meddler's arm
Didn't set out to cause him harm.

Migrant Warblers
When migrant warblers wing their way,
They check the local food's okay.

Mime and Magic
Write me a book every gardener would read:
I'll show you a flower that sprung from a seed.

Missing Birds
It sometimes troubles me to think
Of all the birds I must have missed.

Moggie Manners
A cat behaves in the manner it ought,
And not in the way you think you have taught.

Nectar Quota
Take the wise bee as your prime example:
Restraining greed it just takes a sample.

Nettles
Brushing a nettle you'll feel how it stings;
Crushing it tightly no consequence brings.

Night Owl
When the night sky starts to scowl,
All falls still except the owl.

Octopus
There's remarkably little that's quite so obvious
As all eight arms on a quivering octopus.

Oystercatchers
With waves bearing food almost out of their reach,
Oystercatchers scavenge along the wet beach.

Panda
Among the wonders you'll find in a zoo
Is watching a panda that's chewing bamboo.

Pansies
I love to see pansies peep over a wall:
They always delight one though ever so small.

Pansy Faces
Baskets of pansies with delicate faces
Have greater attraction than airs and graces.

Partridges
In spite of raptors haunting the moors,
Partridges nest in patches of gorse.

Penning
It's hard to get sheep to enter a pen:
They know that they should but can't decide when.

Petals
Each petal to drop reveals an attraction
To whence it came through a fertile reaction.

Phytodiversity
Most plants have potential as medication
Yet suffer the threat of eradication.

Picked Out
Roses show flowers like people speak words;
Only those worthy are picked and preserved.

Pig Food
Where oak trees' acorns litter the ground
Foraging pigs are commonly found.

Pigeons' Problems
While feeding pigeons grow fatter and fatter,
A roaming falcon will cause them to scatter.

Pitiful Flowers
Those pitiful flowers stuck in a jar
Can seldom feel breezes, cramped as they are.

Poplars
Stout poplars that stand in a colonnade
Pretend they're like soldiers out on parade.

Poppies
Poppies are used as tokens of war,
The very thing that we all abhor.

Posturing Peacock
The peacock's posturing's obviously meant
To show the ladies his urgent intent.

Poultry
Free-ranging spry chickens are sure to thrive,
Unlike dire battery-hens, barely alive.

Predation
Albeit carnivores gorge every day,
Predators never outnumber their prey.

Prey Time
Feather and fur, it's true to say,
Often occur as claw and prey.

Prickly Defences
Bramble and thistle and thorns on roses
Sound like cases of nature's neuroses.

Prior Knowledge
The songbirds know without rehearsal
That after fledging comes dispersal.

Recycled
The withering stems of winter's distress
Spring's birds will recycle, weaving their nests.

Rich Berries
That berries are rich is known to thrushes:
They show on beaks and splashes on bushes.

Roaming Ponies
Young Dartmoor ponies see cars as opponents
When stepping out at inopportune moments.

Robin Redbreast
So slim are his legs and tiny his eyes,
Yet the way he fights is quite a surprise.

Rose in Bloom
While the rose is in bloom don't anticipate snow.
Winter comes all too soon; savour summertime's show.

Rose Petals
Wherever roses grow, their pretty petals fade,
Which seems to let us know we all alike are made.

Screaming Seagulls
While gulls keep screaming as if they're deranged,
Between sweet warblers soft notes are exchanged.

Seed Read
Some books on growing from seeds are a racket;
They say to succeed simply read the packet.

Seedlings
Once the flowers on the lawn have flourished and died,
We're left with the seeds that developed inside.

Seeds
When cutting flowers, leave some for seeds:
Propagation's what nature needs.

Shapely Swans
Despite the beaks of bread they take,
The slimline swan retains its shape.

Shooting
It's been said shooting deer was beloved by royals,
But if so it remains a stain on their morals.

Skein
Flocks of geese when in flight are known as a skein,
Though it's hard to explain this unusual name.

Skylark
High in the sky the brave lark sings,
Testing the strength of its fluttering wings.

Smaller Birds
Whether on branches or down on the ground,
The smaller birds are, the more they look round.

Sneaky Cats
It isn't much use chasing cats from your garden:
They're sure to sneak back without saying pardon.

Sows
Happy with piglets or smiling alone,
Sows have a character all of their own.

Sow's Litter
When a sow starts feeding her first-born litter,
The pride in her eyes persuades them to glitter.

Spider Meals
With patterns little altering,
It's meals arrive unfaltering.

Spiky Hedge
The spiky hedge that bounds a field
Keeps birds and insects well concealed.

Spring Robins
Watching robins in spring with fresh feathers endowed,
You'll find two are an item and three make a crowd.

Squirrels and Jays
No sooner squirrels have hidden their store
Than jays start seeking the nuts they adore.

Support
A climbing plant, having much to achieve,
May need a support to which it can cleave.

Survival
Survival of species through alimentation
We have to concede is a cause of predation.

Swallowed Pride
O daffodil, daffodil, swallow your pride:
Pray play me a tune on that trumpet you hide.

Swift Swallow
The early swallow dispatches winter
In flight to match an Olympic sprinter.

Tawny Lullaby
When a tawny owl hoots then gets a reply
It makes less of a call than a lullaby.

Thoughtful Animals
Whenever I've wondered if animals think,
My good old dog's shown me we must have a link.

Thrush Song
Piercing with song a matutinal haze,
We cherish the thrush's precious displays.

Tortoise
A tortoise perambulates
Carrying its carapace.

Value Added
The spiky hedge that bounds the field
Keeps birds and insects well concealed.

Whirling Seagulls
Distant drifts of snowflakes swirling
Soon turn into seagulls whirling.

Wingers and Singers
While most birds prefer to fly on the wing,
Some others have opted to stand and sing.

Woodpigeons
Way in the distance a woodpigeon coos,
Waking its kin in innumerable queues.

Worth the Pain
Fresh nettle-leaves and bramble-fruit
Make gathering a fraught pursuit.

Zoo Vibes
Though a baby baboon was cheeky and chunky,
She fell for the charm of a colobus monkey.

CHAPTER 14 with 62 two-liners

FOOD & DRINK

Advertisements
Among the advertisements classed as the worst
Are some that relate to the quenching of thirst.

Bar Stool
A regular stool in a popular bar
Is much to be envied whoever you are.

Barbies
Heeding females' subtle insinuation,
Barbies made cooking a male recreation.

Barred Maid
She pulled a short pint, and sadly
She told a good joke, but badly.

Beer Cadgers
People who cheat to cadge a free beer
Have their own bulging bellies to fear.

Beer Effects
While feeding their bellies with glasses of beer,
They start to believe all the rubbish they hear.

Beerless
If breweries ceased the production of beer,
The people might find they've less trouble to fear.

Berries
The raspberry carries a surfeit of seeds:
Just maybe that's why the strawberry succeeds.

Breadmakers
Those home appliances, loaf-of-bread makers,
Could put out of work professional bakers.

Breakfast
No, it isn't how good the cereal is,
But whether the packet pleases the kids.

Capped Menu
The host who offers you à la carte
Hasn't yet learnt the 'table d'hôte' art.

Cheese
Those who say cheese is a product of milk
Might stop to wonder if wool comes from silk.

Chefs
When would-be chefs converge in the kitchen,
They'll all show signs of imminent friction.

Chefs on TV
Male TV chefs are attractive to women;
It must be the sight of men in the kitchen.

Chef's Language
A top chef has been known to utter bad language
Watching pâté and houmous filling a sandwich.

Chop-Chop
Onions glaze his stinging eyes:
Fingertips risk a sharp surprise.

Claptrap
Much of the claptrap one hears at the bar
Comes from folk constantly quaffing a jar.

Consumption
Heeding the warnings they issue persistently,
Suggests all I consume really must be bad for me.

Corner Man
He sets up his stall at the corner each week,
Selling fruit and veggies displayed at their peak.

Costly Endorsements
Knowing what extra costs were enforced,
She'd not buy goods that chefs had endorsed.

Decent Diets
Rather too many to chefdom aspire
When decent diets are all we require.

Dinner Discounts
Reductions offered on meals can surprise us:
They might be on portions, rather than prices!

Drink
Drink to cure thirst and drink to prevent it.
Either way drinking's a liquid asset.

Fish Fingers
A tempting helping of tasty fish fingers
With chips and peas are a pleasure that lingers.

Fishy Tale
Allowed to grow beyond their teens,
Young pilchards come as tinned sardines.

Flavour and Taste
Is it right to say flavour differs from taste?
The pundit suggests they're reciprocally based.

Food Waste
Discarding food waste's what councillors suggest:
Putting it onto your compost heap's best.

Foodless
Cancel the dairy, all grain and red meat;
Soon there'll be barely a thing left to eat.

Fresh Tastes
A multiracial breakfast left the store,
Containing tastes she failed to face before.

Fungi
The person who first fresh mushrooms digested
Might have disliked other fungi he tested.

Gastronomy
Chefs' menus will brook no English at all;
Their words are too long and portions too small.

Grapes
Grapes that fall on hard floors will roll away,
But dropped on a rug that's where they will stay.

Hampers and Champers
Her pastoral stories of picnics and hampers
Are still retold using strawberries and champers.

Hiding the Rind
What some stores display as lean bacon's a racket:
Their fatty bits hide at one end of the packet.

High Table
To dine with the gentry can be confusing,
Not knowing which wine or sauce to be choosing.

Hilarity
The laughter of diners grows way past describing,
Their joking promoted by wine they're imbibing!

Kitchen Appliances
Kitchen appliances help us to cook,
Providing we also read the right book.

Know Where
Where the beer flows, there goes he.
How he knows is what beats me!

Laggards
When Friday's laggards at last are turned out,
Beware of the odd incontinent lout.

Larger from Lager
He tends to get increasingly larger,
Yet still can't tell his ale from his lager.

Lettuces
They come to the superstore stuck in plastic:
We prefer from farmer and straight to basket.

Lingering Tastes
The last tastes of repasts, you might have noticed,
Like parting kisses will linger the longest.

Lobster Pots
With empty lobster pots stacked on the quay,
You get a hint of what dinner might be.

Meaningful Menus
An opulent menu is proffered sometimes
To nourish the cells of executive minds.

Multi-buys
Acquire the habit of multi-buy spotting
To lower some prices when you're out shopping.

No Delay
Now decaff coffee has made the grade,
Let's trust dechoc and dehop aren't delayed.

Organic Option
If man won't switch from impure to organic,
We'll have to endure sustainable panic.

Out Shopping
Whenever your shopping becomes a pain,
Remember when menus were all the same.

Parental Guidance
Parental guidance doesn't apply
When parents are absent, boozing nearby.

Peeling
Start peeling an apple and watch it ooze;
The more you peel, the more goodness you lose.

Peelings
When you bake a potato first peel it clean,
For you never can tell where on earth it's been.

Pizza Feature
Some gadgets embody a special feature
That helps you make dough for a home-baked pizza.

Rare Steak
He ordered his fillet really rare,
But not so rare it was hardly there!

Sausage Sandwich
If you slice a sausage to put in your sandwich,
Spray tomato ketchup to act as a garnish.

Size Effects
Eating impinges on physical size;
Its dutiful counterpart's exercise.

Splashing Out
From teacups in cafes the brew splashes out,
And doubtless it's due to their pots' silly spouts.

Subtlety
Their sandwich is a subtle feat
Of hiding what we thought we'd eat.

Sustenance
Fried rice is China's favourite dish:
The Englishman relishes chips and fish.

Thirst
Exceeding the need for liquid ingestion,
Thirst is a yearning beyond invention.

Toper's Tale
After he'd conquered his enemy, booze,
He'd only his old pot belly to lose.

Unnatural Veg
Tomatoes with skin akin to leather
Have been deprived of natural weather.

The Waiting Game
Always remember the head waiter's name,
So you can use it to bolster your fame.

CHAPTER 15 with 21 two-liners

FRIENDSHIP

Bad Friends
When your good friends turn bad,
Bless the good times you had.

Candid Advice
He always disliked the need to rely on
Advice acquired from a candid companion.

Companions
No matter what motives dictate dogs' actions,
There's no denying they make good companions.

Company
In later days you'll come to see
The treasure that's good company.

Dab Hand
A friendly dab hand at all forms of plumbing
Sadly's a person who's seldom forthcoming.

Enrolling
When joining a club, if you're asked to enroll
It's just to ensure things are under control.

The Epigram Man
Dispensing his wit wherever he can,
He's known by friends as the epigram man.

False Friend
Beware the false friend disguising a foe:
The high five hiding a blow from below.

Friends
It's nice to have friends who are glad when you're right
And lend their support when you're feeling contrite.

Friendship
A friendship's inferred by the person's own presence,
Assuming it's always preferred to their absence.

Good Relations
Being reconciled with a party displeased
Is one of those pleasures most keenly received.

Isolation
Through families and friends we escape desolation,
Yet each of us lives in our own isolation.

Joy on Meeting
Keep us apart a week at least;
Joy on meeting is thus increased.

Kindness
The less you expect of people you know,
The more you respect the kindness they show.

Natural Aptitude
Natural aptitude comes at a price:
It leads to your friends requesting advice.

Neighbourly Kindness
Bless the kind neighbours whose place is adjacent,
About your well-being they don't rest complacent.

New Friends
Success ensuing from making new friends
Depends on how long the friendship extends.

Peer Group
A regular peer group from various trades
Goes out to view birds through their optical aids.

Pets and People
Pamper your poodle, converse with the cat;
Neighbours could do with attention like that.

Reunion
Fifty years on, a reunion traces
The remnants of once-familiar faces.

Soulmates
The friend who accepts how one fails and succeeds
Is the sort of soulmate everyone needs.

CHAPTER 16 with 22 two-liners

GENETICS

Adaptation
Adaptation's the motor of evolution,
Each subtle adjustment a driven solution.

Ancestors
From branches and twigs on the family tree,
We discover the sources of you and me.

Apples and Pears
The pear and the apple, each separately dwells,
Both carefully keeping their genes to themselves.

Condescension
If condescension were blessed with a twin,
The gene of meanness would surely creep in.

Darwin's Loss
Darwin said Shakespeare made him feel nauseous;
The bard would have scorned the gene of his coarseness.

DNA
Deoxyribonucleic acid
Is DNA in language less vapid.

Dogs
Dogs with moustaches and elephant ears
Show what happens when man interferes.

Family Trees
People spend fortunes tracing their line;
I was fortunate, Darwin did mine.

Gene Flow
Progression of genes was only one-way
Until geneticists entered the fray.

Generations
One thing we tend to underestimate
Is what new generations generate.

Genetic Benefits
For genetic gifts of distinguishing traits
We stay indebted, be they seldom retraced.

Genetic Chatter
Talking too much, not thinking enough, it seems
Is probably something that comes with the genes.

Genetic Destiny
It's known that genes can disclose our destiny
In ways beyond those of physiognomy.

Genetic Identity
Maybe loopholes of extra complexity
Pose a threat to genetic identity.

Genetic Migration
A nation's desires embrace immigration:
It serves to prevent genetic stagnation.

Migration
As emigrants ebb and immigrants flow,
The gene sea fluctuates, to and fro.

Natural Selection
When men select from new women they've seen,
They're stirred by the same immutable gene.

Nature's Mystery
The inner working of nature's mystery
Isn't revealed in the tomes of history.

Revolution
Evolution produces gradual change:
Revolution obtains a rapid exchange.

Smallest Fingers
The ultimate species that lingers
Will be that with the smallest fingers.

Source of Species
To a simple gel of bits and pieces
Some still attribute the source of species.

Speedy Evolution
Mankind, in a trice, can change a dove's feather;
The ant and the antelope took forever.

CHAPTER 17 with 58 two-liners

GOVERNMENT

Anarchy
For fear of anarchy's hideous ills,
We inflict a government on ourselves.

Backup
When statesmen make their voices heard,
Their close advisers vet each word.

Balance of Powers
Stable nations have checks and balances;
Power unfettered is where the malice is.

Ballot
A country's minority tends to be right;
The majority, though, possesses the might.

Ballot v Bullet
Where voters express free choice at the ballot,
Democracy rues those ruled by the bullet.

Budget Time
The government's budget, still unrevealed,
Arouses dread of some trick they've concealed.

Centralism
Centralisation concentrates power;
People's control is therefore the lower.

Chancellors
Some chancellors fancy the confidence route:
Economists forecast what's nearer the truth.

Clean Sweep
The gutters are swept where councillors bide:
It's all a matter of where you reside.

Coin a Phrase
Our Dear Prince Charles, when you next see the Queen
Please ask if your coin need read 'Ich Dien'.

Consuls
A consul shows others his country's best side,
And leaves them believing he wouldn't have lied.

Correctness
MPs' behaviour, we've a right to expect,
Should always remain politically correct.

Councillors
Canvassing councillors play the fiddle:
Promising much, delivering little.

Democracy
Democracy only properly functions
Because the good 'uns outnumber the bad 'uns.

Dictums
Politicians risk speaking with such conviction
They start to believe their erroneous dictums.

Diplomat
One asset a diplomat has to refine
Is quickly interpreting signs of the time.

Disorder
Disorder arises from lack of controls,
A state which, perversely, meets anarchy's goals.

Dysfunction
Democratic dysfunction
Falls prey to corruption.

Elections
Voting fervour grips the nation
More in hope than expectation.

Electoral Froth
Drop the orations, the lies and the froth;
Stop the elections, I want to get off.

A Fine Distinction
The Lords is a house with lords within it:
Lord's is the home of the men of cricket.

First Among Equals
First among equals? Not Tony Blair,
As his Cabinet stooges would swear!

Foreign Affairs
Ministerial records of foreign affairs
Store intimate details of secretive heirs.

Freedom and Power
Belief in freedom reveals compassion;
Achieving power sees no such concession.

Governing Britain
Governing multicultural Britain
Means retreating from ancient tradition.

Having Our Say
While there are statutes we have to obey,
Only at polling we're given our say.

High Positions
It's not beyond doubt that politicians
Use the nation to hike their positions.

Laughs
Despite the gaffes that MPs make,
They make us laugh with votes at stake.

Manifestation
Distorted manifestos confirm
How fickle politicians can turn.

Members of Parliament
For most of the time they seem locked in disputes;
When they've lost people's trust they're back in cahoots.

Mixed Methods
A business abjures what's non-pragmatic:
MPs adhere to methods dogmatic.

Monarchy
The business of monarchy's likely to turn
Its partnerships into a family firm.

Names Matter
For top politicians who visit abroad,
Being deemed a statesman is ample reward.

Our Queen
However widely and often she strays,
Our Queen engenders the warmest of praise.

Out of Kilter
When policy's pendulum strains its range,
Imbalance in government augurs change.

Parliamentary Contrivance
They rise in the House with every intention
Of raising support by argumentation.

Parliamentary Levies
Parliamentary representation
Legalizes infernal taxation.

Political Decisions
Our local unqualified politicians
Are trusted with making national decisions.

Political Hustles
Playing the game of political hustles,
Britain shames her name by bedding with Brussels.

Political Parties
When Tories get bored with social pretences,
They start playing games with Labour's back benches.

Politicians
Count how many MPs this country sustains:
We require far fewer but more with some brains.

Politics
Functioning solely with voter-compliance,
Politics serves neither art nor science.

Polling
Discounting the tactics and voting through proxies,
In the end it comes down to crosses in boxes.

Pollster Control
When pollsters collect self-evident data,
They'll need analysis sooner than later.

Poor Attenders
MPs aren't keen on attendance, it seems,
Preferring to watch on their laptop screens.

Premiers
A premier's major success consists in
Giving his ministers leave to assist him.

Premiers' Problems
The old year waned and yawned at things to come
While unresolved problems still maundered on.

Propositions
A government party in opposition
Finds it effective to test propositions.

Representation
Proportional representation relies
On sorting MPs by the hue of their ties.

Risk-takers
The risks those elected precariously take
Don't haunt them despite the mistakes they might take.

Silent Guy
One contemplates a pleasant land,
A haven where Guy Fawkes is banned.

Subsidization
Some government ailings, in many a nation,
Are fixed by injections called subsidization.

Taxation
Taxation's a pain the Chancellor distributes;
The cure is the gain that he claims as tributes.

Tremors
When heads of state traverse the planet,
The good earth shakes, and all those on it.

Tyranny
Tyrannous government, wicked and cruel,
Follows the fall of legality's rule.

Vexations
Vexations for which politicians are noted
Arise when bad bits from old speeches are quoted.

Weal and Will
To the country's weal our leaders aspire,
Transcending the will of common desire.

WSC
The vote that he lost was a blow they dealt,
Like hitting a boxer below the belt.

CHAPTER 18 with 43 two-liners

HEALTH

Addiction
Cannabis feeds the needs of addiction;
Poverty offers a safe prediction.

Alien Defences
Swearing that chemicals damaged his senses,
He cursed his pills as alien defences.

Antiseptic
To check if a sedative's not antiseptic,
A pharmacist's doubtless the best to inspect it.

Back Date
The state of your lumbar region's important,
So make a date with old Doctor Deportment.

Birthing
The role of a father needs seminal sources:
The toll on a mother needs greater resources.

Blossom Pollen
In blossom time when pollen blows,
Allergic symptoms irk the nose.

Body Warners
Our bodies will warn us, through pain and aching,
When something we're doing clearly needs changing.

Bouts of Laughter
A bout of laughter's more catching than flu:
Rather more healthy, and pleasanter, too.

Careful
No matter how careful you think that you are,
Your body can tell when you're going too far.

Crick in the Neck
If you're shifting gear from ahead to reverse,
A crick in the neck on occasion occurs.

Cures
Intelligence claims, with scant dissension,
Cures will often be worse than prevention.

Dentist
You must tell the young dentist who comes through the doors
That it isn't *his* mouth, it's emphatically *yours*.

Dentistry
Students should pause before being a dentist;
It's an inside job with tiny prosthetics.

Exercise
Strict exercise aims at physical fitness,
And priming the mind's no less efficacious.

Eyewash
It's all very well saying eyewash is nonsense:
Cleansing one's eyes is a sensible process.

Fine Fettle
Keep rotating those bicycle pedals
So that you'll thrive in ultra-fine fettle.

Fresh Air
Of all things normally kept out of doors,
Fresh air should be welcomed inside, of course.

Get Up and Go
Energy follows a good night's sleep:
Lethargy echoes late hours we keep.

Go-getter
Lacking the rests of an underused secretary,
Her overstressed brain's reached negative equity.

Good Health
For overall health in old age to prevail,
Both mind and body must counter betrayal.

Handy Packets
Those handy packets of twenty to smoke
Used to show people how best they could choke.

Health of the Nation
Medicine won't save the health of the nation:
Healthier food outplays medication.

Healthy Laughter
Far healthier than making some worrisome gaffe,
Is taking the tonic of having a laugh.

Healthy Player
A picture of health, sound in wind and limb,
He was always fit to boot the ball in.

Impurity
Impurity stems from contamination,
Often imputed to lax sanitation.

Joints
Old joints incurring articulation
Feel sorely in need of recuperation.

Lethargy
A bout of lackadaisical lethargy
Comes about by a lacking of energy.

Mastication
Master the action of mastication
And find satisfaction in faster digestion.

Medication's Train
Once you're aboard medication's train,
The signals show 'Not stopping again'.

Moisture Control
Taking control of excessive aridity
Helps one maintain a healthy humidity.

Mother's Motto
A growing boy derives his strength
From exercise and nutriment.

Nicks
If razor blades were made too keen,
We'd need more antiseptic cream.

Overeating
Believing that eating's your reason for living
Could easily lead to distressing misgivings.

Panacea
In bouts of distress, excess spirit, they fear,
May sadly be used as a panacea.

Passenger Pleasure
A bicycle's passenger earns the pleasure
Of keeping in trim whatever the weather.

Pointed Problems
Pointed shoes, the podiatrist knows,
Promise problems to innocent toes.

Rehab
Those in need of rehab are mostly well known,
Though one fears they can't leave narcotics alone.

Remedies
Chemical remedies - tainted parodies -
Lack the clear notes of nature's pure melodies.

Sneezing
When you find you constantly have to sneeze,
In means that your nostrils are ill at ease.

Stress
Your heartbeats can tell if you're suffering stress,
And if that should occur start worrying less.

Sugar and Salt
Here's how to tell sugar and salt apart:
One ruins your teeth, the other your heart.

Tension's Strength
Tension can stretch ourselves nearly to breaking,
Despite the attempts at relaxing we're taking.

Wellness
Purveyors of medicine deal mainly with illness;
Their task could be eased by promotion of wellness.

CHAPTER 19 *with 33 two-liners*

HISTORY

Antiques
Antiques are relics of centuries past
Which challenge today to make things that last.

Archaeologist
He found his scraping exasperating:
Preferring to work on carbon dating.

Archaeology
The peaceable past no foe can invade,
Save archaeology's trowel and spade.

Artefacts
Innumerable artefacts stay concealed,
Although they're patiently being revealed.

The Book of Past Ages
The book of past ages, with stories untold,
Is bound to be opened as pages unfold.

Central Heating
Roman villas were heated with hypocausts
Which later took many and various sorts.

Clumsiness
Clumsiness adds to the price of antiques:
The fewer there are, the higher it creeps.

Deeds
No valiant deed outlives its doer:
Only its record endures, as prover.

Diggers
During the war we'd all dig for victory;
Archaeologists dig, but now it's for history.

Effete Repeats
Like effete repeats we see on TV,
The present rehearses its history.

Global Birth
The mystery of global birth
Is only known to mother earth.

Historians
Aeons of history the ancients forsook
Need more than historians to open their book.

Historic Beauty
Most people in Britain accept a position
Where beauty competes with historic tradition.

Historical Sources
Conflicting reports appearing in papers
Drag historians through all sorts of capers.

Historiography
Historiographers write up history:
How they do it is often a mystery.

History
History teaches of wars and their dates
Instead of the folly of human mistakes.

History Book
History isn't a copy of what's to come;
The past is a yarn that's already been spun.

History's Tally
Ardent historians may disagree strongly,
But history's mostly of things done wrongly.

Kept Ephemera
Although ephemera aren't meant to last,
When some have been kept they can tell of the past.

Invasions
Many deep and extensive excavations
Show Britain's been prone to foreign invasions.

Leeway
History's written by folk who weren't there;
They must have a deal of leeway to spare.

Letters
Ephemeral letters, by chance discovered,
Replace lost moments now safely recovered.

Living's Encyclopedia
The story of man's mistakes and misgivings
Would fill an encyclopedia of living.

Megaliths
Britain's collections of standing stones
Stand cultures apart from cars and phones.

Nail-biting
Judging by statues from mythical tales,
Romans and Greeks must have bitten their nails.

Outmatched
Impressively versed in historical facts,
He'd leave his converser completely outmatched.

Pen and Ink
Given the changes, it's hard now to think
We once wrote our words with a pen and ink.

Personal Journals
Fertile with notes and hints of temerity,
Personal journals wink at posterity.

Plebs
Looking way way back to a different aeon,
Britain's population was mainly plebeian.

Retro
Retro pertains to the recent past,
Some of which now might leave us aghast.

Ruins
Ruins are something all countries preserve.
Often as quality-lessons they serve.

Senses Enough
Primitive man made senses suffice
Without recourse to money or vice.

Sherds
Trivial sherds of ancient pottery
Serve as treasure in archaeology.

CHAPTER 20 with 14 two-liners

HOBBIES

Board Games
Once hand-held devices had interfered,
It meant that old board games soon disappeared.

Cameras
A lens mayn't record what we thought we saw:
Some shutters won't catch what we caught before.

Fisherman
While constantly casting, watching and praying,
The fisherman sits there, reeling and baiting.

Gardening
Refrain from gardening unless you've the knack
Of bending down without straining your back.

Hobbies
While the oldest profession is as they say,
The oddest of hobbies is shopping, today!

Jigsaw
When a puzzle consists of a thousand pieces,
The pain in your back with each session increases.

Obsession
For any collector, the urge of possession
Could quickly become a fraught obsession.

Patterns
Occasionally patterns outwit the knitter,
As painters might fail to depict a sitter.

Philately
We've seen a decline in global philately,
Due to less usage of postage stamps latterly.

Positive Negative
A positive role the negative played
For photos in old pre-digital days.

Pressure of Progress
The pleasure of knitting is slipping away,
The pressure of progress too hard to gainsay.

Puzzling
While difficult puzzles demand contemplation,
Finding answers repays with gratification.

Snapshots
Often old snapshots make past times recur
A great deal better than in truth they were.

Tea Cosy
His cosy owes a great deal to its maker,
Her crochet still wearing so many years later.

CHAPTER 21 with 27 two-liners

HOLIDAYS

Beaches
Beaches appear in everyone's dream,
From young to old and those in between.

Comfort Zone
Escaping the bounds of one's comfort zone
Adds a dimension to being back home.

Conversations
A dialogue on their latest vacation's
The softest option for conversations.

Cruises
Drifting around on some faraway cruise,
Their beautiful land they choose to abuse.

English Vacation
While fitful sunshine flits behind clouds,
People on beaches shiver in crowds.

Enjoyment
Bright moments kept from year to year
Make vapid meantimes disappear.

Foreign Liaisons
Dating abroad with romantic ideas
More likely than not will end up in tears.

Hankering
Though holidays refresh our minds,
We hanker after left-behinds.

Holiday Brochure
They said that we'd see some amazing places;
Their glossy brochure is where the disgrace is.

Holidaymakers
Holidaymakers send us their pictures,
Letting us know they're the luckiest critters.

Lost Souls
Many holiday lets, once homely cottages,
Are heartless investments in soulless villages.

New Tickles
How many pebbles will tickle new toes?
Nobody counts them, so nobody knows.

Odd Holidays
How oddly holidays trouble a mind,
Unable to help what's been left behind.

Old Brits on Tour
They've been on a tour of overseas places,
And still they're wearing brown boots and striped braces!

Phoneless Holiday
When your loved ones have gone without their phone,
They yearn for their rapid return back home.

Picture Postcards
Picture postcards we send, and those we receive,
Forever choose skies we can hardly believe.

Plus ça Change
Hooray, hooray for the seaside brigade:
They've stayed in love with the bucket and spade.

Quoits
Where people on beaches are lying relaxing,
The flinging of quoits can be more than distracting.

Rainy Vacations
Those rainy occasions when on vacation
Are meant for consuming the books we've taken.

Sand
What's the attraction of sand on a beach?
It tells you that work is well out of reach

Sandy Reaches
Chicks who've lain on summer beaches
Blame sandy grains for nether itches.

Seaside Delights
Beside all the pleasures the seaside claims
Are screaming seagulls and low aeroplanes.

Tents
They wake as houses for holiday weeks:
The rest of the year they curl up and sleep.

Tourists
Tourists reporting their pseudo-exploring
Merit their ranking among the most boring.

Trippers
Visitors daily come and go,
Mimicking tidal high and low.

Vacation Evaluation
We're often persuaded to visit abroad;
At least we can test if the ads were a fraud.

Visits to Go
Though many countries have places worth seeing,
With each year's visits the number's receding.

CHAPTER 22 with 11 two-liners

HOPE & EMOTIONS

Alleviation
Alleviation of worry or pain
Embraces the hope it can be sustained.

Alone
'Alone' engenders ambivalent notions:
Contentment and sadness its mixed emotions.

Frisson
Albeit we're innocent, uniforms prompt
A frisson of challenge we'll need to confront.

Hope
Expectation takes hope too far:
Hoping still leaves the door ajar.

Hope and Memory
Memory always looks over its shoulder:
Hope for ever emboldens its owner.

Hope for Sale
Hope is sold as a shop commodity
Where it's known as cosmetics commonly.

Hoping
Hope's an emotion that keeps us going,
A spur that ensures we go on hoping.

Remembrance
An aching heart will not forget:
It must remember and regret.

Scorn that Shows
When spoken emotions falter, forlorn,
A facial expression conveys one's scorn.

Virtual Certainty
Brimming with anticipation,
Hope disguises expectation.

Vital Choice
The heart that's facing a grave affair
Must choose between courage and despair.

CHAPTER 23 with 15 two-liners

HUMANKIND

Anthropologists
Across the continents' open spaces
Anthropologists study the races.

Complication
Complication's the nature of humans' lives;
Our coeval creatures need but to survive.

Credits and Debits
Mankind credits nature with waving wheat
But cavils at animals eating meat.

Humane Change
The world's in change, still it stays the same
And won't improve till it's more humane.

Humankind
Humankind started with most people fools
Until they began to learn nature's rules.

Inequality
All souls are equal upon arrival,
Differing only beyond survival.

Misguided Mankind
Misguided mankind, explorer of space,
Return to concerns of the human race!

Morals
Soon we'll have left all morals behind;
Such is the folly of humankind.

No Blame or Shame
No shame's involved if you have a fine frame;
If you're oddly built, no guilt can pertain.

Primordial Creatures
They crawled from the sea, primordial creatures
Adapting their forms to fit nature's niches.

Ranks
From baron to earl, and ranks preceding,
None shall prevail over human being.

Simply Living
Envy those who lived when Earth was thought flat:
They slept, fed and mated - and that was that!

Soul
The human soul is the essence of man,
Ever-enduring since living began.

Space Raid Shelters
The safest protection from outraged space
Is biodomes built for the human race.

Thinking
The gift of thinking distinguishes man
From other species, unable to plan.

CHAPTER 24 with 178 two-liners

HUMOUR

Annoyance
It isn't much fun, you have to admit,
When a prize is won by a perfect twit.

Artificiality
Artificial this, and ersatz for that;
Next we'll be fixing fake fur on the cat.

Banana Tunnel
Mainly due to the use of a polytunnel,
We now grow bananas without any trouble.

Bequeathing
After death her bequest wasn't hers to give, still
The donation was given by someone called Will.

Big Cats
Lions and tigers are known as big cats:
Might they have been over-eating, perhaps?

Billionaire
Never try phoning a billionaire;
It's a billion to one he won't be there.

Biodegradability
No bio degrades quite so well as
The monkey-fruit's yellow pyjamas.

Boys and Girls
Little girls have complexions like peaches and cream;
Little boys collect traces of places they've been.

Budgie Homes
A wry recidivist said of judges
Their wigs would make great nests for grey budgies.

Butterflies
Should you see butterflies forming a queue,
It may be because they've some shopping to do.

Carbon Jet
It speeds near space but like the snail
To flee disgrace it leaves a trail.

Catching Up
Philosophers told us flat earth was round;
Next they'll be telling us coffee is ground.

Centipede
A centipede scaling a garden wall
Is bound to think it's a hundred feet tall.

Chicken
When the head of a chicken appears through a crack,
There's no chance in the world of it turning right back.

Climate Change
Should global warming melt Bangkok,
We'd need our sunblock round the clock.

Closet
It's usually easy to visit a closet
But occasionally hard to leave a deposit.

Compensation
While scribbled addresses can leave them confused,
Those joke-chosen postcards keep posties amused.

Coverage
Her figure's revealed as up with the best:
It's quite ironic the coverage she gets!

Cowboys
Now very few cowboys are using lassos,
They've taken to giving home owners the blues.

Creature Comforts
Creature comforts embrace a package of features
From cushions for cats to cassocks for preachers.

Cricket to Come
Conceive what tomorrow's umpire befalls:
Intelligent wickets and talking balls.

Cup and Saucer
If you just imagine a cup and a saucer,
It's seldom the latter that sits on the former.

Daring
Desert safari or rigorous diet?
Each great to be on, if you dare to try it.

Deadpan
His deadpan patter was quaintly beguiling:
It seemed he'd not mastered vocalized smiling.

Dear Wife
When a husband refers to 'my dear wife',
She's overpriced or the love of his life.

Decimal Point
When deducing the root of a big mistake,
The decimal dot has its own point to make.

Dental Tension
Two not readily reconciled:
The dentist and the crocodile.

Design Brief
Were horses designed
With buttocks in mind?

Diplomacy
Remembering her birthday is diplomatic:
Disclosing her age is more problematic.

Disgruntlements
When rude disgruntlements get on one's wick,
Using complaint forms might just do the trick.

Disparity
Up to the belfry the choirboy's note floats;
Down in the lilies the courting frog croaks.

Dolphins
It's said dolphins smile as they leap from water
Because they're all after the captain's daughter.

Epsoms
Epsom colts are raised for the racing:
Epsom salts are preferred for purging.

Expectation
We expect good and bad all living together
In much the same way as we do with the weather.

Extremities
Extremities are always first to get cold,
Like fingers and toes, or a prominent nose.

Facial Intrusion
The jerk who invented shaving men's faces
Deserves a place in the book of disgraces.

Faking It
Little's harder to fake than a laugh
When a joke isn't funny by half.

Faux Pas
The knight withdrew a sword from the stone;
Alas, he'd left his scabbard at home.

Fear or Favour
Pessimists fear some improbable sin;
Optimists favour a lottery win.

Flaked
He cast his eyes on the barber's floor
And saw the snow, not present before.

Flute Concerto
The strings and the wind were soaring aloft
When out in the heavens the flautist coughed!

Flying Time
When we want to think that time isn't flying,
It somehow seems that our clocks aren't trying.

The Food Chain
When a thrush takes a worm, its concern is that
It might just, in its turn, fall prey to a cat.

Forlornness
One day when feeling completely forlorn,
He stripped the strawberries then painted the lawn.

Freedom
He who escapes to his potting shed
Knows there's an hour of freedom ahead.

Funny Business
Something that's funny can leave one amused,
Otherwise feeling completely confused.

Gateposts
Gateposts are used by a tipsy Alsatian
Less for support than a swift micturation.

Gents
When they see 'Gentlemen' over the door,
I hope that foreigners know what it's for.

Grapefruit
How did the grapefruit stem from the grape?
Maybe Darwin had made a mistake.

Hasty Lady Cyclist
She sat on a saddle as wide as a chair,
But flew down the hills on a wing and a prayer.

Height Matters
When seeking a mate, she reminded herself
He ought to be taller to reach the top shelf.

Hint, Hint
He spent the day with a hint on his head:
The comb she'd borrowed still lay on her bed.

His Hair
She simply adored his jet black hair,
And wished he'd more of them here and there.

Hot Drinks
If you've hot drinks with a tray on your lap,
Try to ensure you don't stop for a nap.

Hot-water Bottle
The rubber bottle he filled with hot water
Does more for cold feet than the socks he bought her.

How Come?
An oval track, a rectangular ground;
And yet all the runners go round and round.

Humour
A sense of humour can mitigate stress:
As laughter increases, worry gets less.

In the Pink
Find her a lover who'll find her a drink,
And like a flamingo she's in the pink.

Interstices
Interstices occupy tiny spaces;
Smaller, it seems, than the length of their name is.

It Figures
Moustached statisticians fancy their chances
With numerate ladies hirsute in their fancies.

Jetskis
Respectively noisy and looking real silly,
Jetskis compare to a toad on a lily.

Jockey
The amorous jockey won the last laugh
When he walked his mare down the bridal path.

Jokes
Making jokes is not of necessity flippant:
Their way of explaining things plainly efficient.

Kangaroos
It's said kangaroos are found in Australia,
As if to imply they get lost in that area.

Keep Faith
Don't rashly lose faith in the whole human race!
You still have some millions to vet, face to face.

Laces
Laces enable your shoes to fit nicely,
Provided you tighten them up precisely.

Lachrymose Gulls
No matter how hard you keep going on trying,
It seems you will never stop seagulls from crying.

Last Collar
Now the vicar's last dog is no longer there,
He's the only one with a collar to wear.

Laughing
Laughing's a noisier manner of smiling
Though seldom, if ever, quite so beguiling.

Laughter Hereafter
Ensure you savour your measure of laughter:
Such flippant pursuit mayn't suit the hereafter.

Laundry
Hang out the washing with pegs on the line:
So often it's yours, infrequently mine.

Long Weekends
The long weekends that he'd marked confidential
Were really short stays with endless potential.

Lookalikes
So how do you tell two robins apart?
Methinks it must be an avian art.

Lucky Balls
For Lottery winners the luck of the draw
Depends on small balls bouncing through a small door.

Matching Outfits
At the nudist convention I guessed
I'd be wearing the same as the rest.

Mates
High usage of 'mate' I'd never have known,
Except for men's use of the mobile phone.

Men and Women
Men take more of an interest in women
Than vice versa, for some odd reason.

Messing About
Dressed to impress, we divest for caressing:
Animals manage without all that messing.

Midges
The aerial midge isn't really malicious,
It's just that it finds your blood so nutritious.

Mnemonics
To aid recall, create a mnemonic;
Then, above all, try not to forget it.

Mongrel Dog
If a mongrel dog had been told whence it came,
It would even now have good cause to complain.

Monkey Antics
She feared she was heading for certain disaster
As, faster and faster, the monkey swung past her.

Muchness
Few people know what a muchness is:
It's muchly the same as sameness is.

Mushrooms
Mushrooms are odd in dispensing with roots,
And landing at night with white parachutes.

Nail Clipping
There's nothing more pleasing than clipping your nails
Except for displaying the skill that entails.

Nappies
Nappies are used to keep babies clean,
Although they're among the dirtiest things seen.

Nature Reserves
A nature reserve is not a location
To run your spaniel or spotted dalmatian.

Nautical Name
One might think that her ladyship goes out sailing:
If not, then her nautical name needs explaining.

Old Masters
Old mistresses can't compete with old masters
In looking attractive to rich investors.

On and In
You hop on a bus and jump in a car.
Try switching them round: they sound most bizarre.

On Approval
He found, from his earlier cavorting,
On approval's the best way of courting.

On Line
Your washing-line has tales to tell
Of things that didn't go so well.

One in Four
Remembering the leap year's turn
I'm pleased to say's not my concern.

Only Proper
It's never the snail that leaps the frog,
Nor ever the tail that wags the dog.

Opencast
Some people recall things so quickly at times,
It's as if they're possessed of opencast minds.

Options
Once monkeys had opted to alter,
Their sages sloped off to Gibraltar.

Orientation
You'll not find a squirrel lost in a forest,
And never see one with a map, I promise.

Palimpsest
The lady withdrew from his bed, distressed;
He calls her replacement his palimpsest.

Penguins
Penguins are birds that go strutting along
But haven't been known to burst into song.

Perspiration
Runners perspire in pursuit of their best:
Creditors sweat to recover bad debts.

Plotless and Witless
Her latest novel was so uninspiring
Even the characters started expiring.

Plum Elite
Plum designations betoken elite;
For apricot jobs one wouldn't compete.

Pony Tails
Bound polo-ponies' tails wave in the air:
No dignity there for the lady mare!

Poor Dog
Such a shame for a dog that's in disgrace:
It hasn't a way of hiding its face.

Posers
Elegant swans impressively feathered
Prepare for photos despite the weather.

Potential Parents
Potential mothers dislike men's pyjamas:
They tend to inhibit potential fathers.

Presumption
If walls have ears belonging to spies,
On keeping mum one's secret relies.

Prime Rhyme
All poets must notice, when reaching their prime,
That skirt and alert make a natural rhyme.

Prime Time
He didn't need sheep to coax him to sleep:
He'd snore throughout the Prime Minister's speech.

Procrastination
Procrastination's the bane of decision;
Its favoured possession's a fence to sit on.

Proof of ID
Next year you'll require your password and PIN
To get a fresh round of beverage in.

Professors
It's odd that professors are given a chair:
After all they can buy them any old where.

Pullovers and Jumpers
Tidy's the pullover, shipshape and neat;
Sloppy the jumper that reaches your feet.

Punctures
Taking his kit for repairing a puncture,
The cyclist sets off on a rubbery adventure.

Pursuit of Girls
He was taught the pursuit of elusive girls
Would be even more fraught than diving for pearls.

Question Time
Having heard his last speech that reason forsook,
My first thought was this: 'Would I purchase his book?'

Queuers
Whether they're patient is not worth debating:
Everyone knows it's the waiting they're hating.

Quiche
A quiche is a flan with fillings on pastry:
A chef is a man with drizzlings quite tasty.

Raindrops
When raindrops descend so terribly heavily,
The way they do it is nothing but cleverly.

Raw Speed
It's always the tortoise, never the worm:
As to raw speed, they're of equal concern.

Real Estate
That real-estate dwelling, the surface of Earth,
Was offered as waters surrounded by turf.

Recycling
Recycling is sometimes misunderstood:
You can't make a tree from planks of wood.

Recycling Patrols
In the cause of recycling, among other things
They'll be making patrols on their motorized bins.

Redundancy
The length of a magpie's tail was inspired:
Now we have pens it's no longer required.

Reminiscing
At times when you find yourself reminiscing,
It's only because letter c's gone missing.

Renamed
They changed his name soon after the marriage,
Referring to him as Sir Plus Baggage.

Replacements
After several years things need replacing,
Except for the missus I'm still embracing.

Rollers
The breaking waves topple then roll to the shore,
Like broken potato-bags spill on the floor.

Rotors
A helicopter sounds like a drill
Creating holes for the clouds to fill.

Sailor
The need of a sailor is, oddly, not swimming
But finding nice ports, with amenable women.

Scarecrows
Rows of scarecrows once looked like farmers
Standing out in their straw pyjamas.

Scientific Solutions
Requesting science to find a solution
Equates to reversing nuclear fusion.

Seagulls
When seagulls start gathering over your head,
You know silly people are tossing them bread.

Shoe Blues
Joseph's coat had numerous hues,
But no one's boned up on his shoes!

Shopping
Said the vendor: 'The buyer is always right.'
Said the buyer: 'He's a pretender, alright.'

Simplest Pleasure
The simplest of pleasures one cannot ignore
Is crunching an apple right down to the core.

Ski Schemer
Though off-piste he believed he could trust her,
She skied off with the Swedish instructor.

Sleuthing for Truth
Disdaining lies, ask any good sleuth,
Wine's sublime at exuding the truth.

Slippy
Up in the branches, its forked tongue jutting,
The cobra dropped as it lost its footing.

Smiling Sow
A somnolent sow points ears at her snout,
And smiles at what only sows know about.

Snooker
Snooker is soothing, absorbing for two,
Just poking at balls with chalk on one's cue.

Songster
A good memory's required by a singing bird:
If it loses the tune it could drop off its perch.

Speculation
If life arose from primordial ooze,
It might subside through inordinate booze.

Spider
It weaves a hammock that *we* call a web,
Then hangs around and expects to be fed.

Spider Problem
A spider's problem was feeding at night,
So it surfed the web for a brighter site.

Spiders Colliding
Out at night when a spider decides to hide,
The chance is it might with another collide.

Starbright
A backward star converts to rats;
How bright are even backward rats!

Station Clock
The station clock with a face on each side
Shows that the time-keeper's nothing to hide.

Stuffing
Kapok is used as stuffing for cushions;
Capons are stuffed with sage and onions.

Sultry
Weather-wise, sultry feels hot and sticky;
Otherwise, passionate's more the ticket.

Sunseeker
She flopped on the sand where the sea didn't reach,
Like a flipperless seal hauled up on a beach.

Swans
Swans contort their necks and primp each feather,
Ready for photos despite the weather.

Syntax
His line on language was rather thin,
Believing syntax a tax on sin.

Taking Flowers
The trouble with taking bunches of flowers is
Knowing if or not they've got empty vases.

Tax
The law for exacting tax from the nation
Must have been passed by a crass population.

Tennis Net
For days when it's intermittently rained,
Only the net has patiently remained.

Tentative Guests
'How good to see you,' we say at the door,
Wondering what we invited them for.

To a Teenager
You're best to rise without delay,
For breakfast comes but once a day!

Tonsils
Here's to the national elections we bore;
Never were so many tonsils so sore.

Too High
Spider, spider up the wall,
Please take care that you don't fall.

Toothy Risk
Chomping and chewing, we only can pray
Our vulnerable tongue keeps out of harm's way.

Torrential Rain
With a dirty car you can hardly complain
If you're facing a drop of torrential rain.

Touching Wood
To ward off bad luck, we tend to touch wood;
Some touch their heads, but aren't sure if they should!

Transparency
Most women look better in see-through clothes
Than ever they would if fully exposed.

Udder Comfort
The milking-cow has a lot to support,
But only lies down as a last resort.

Underground
Carrots and radishes shun the sky,
Preferring to bide where worms pass by.

Unlucky in Love
Prismatic, curvaceous, his choice never varies;
But chasing such rainbows belongs to the fairies!

Varicose Rails
He swore that the rails at the crossings for trains
Bore some of the looks of his varicose veins.

Variety
I find all rabbits the same to my eyes:
Unlike we humans, each one a surprise!

Vox Pop
The voice of the public's an odd how-d'ye-do:
The chips of the many, the fish of the few.

War Applause
Figure the world with a sequence of wars;
Like the Olympics we'd thrive on applause.

The Winner
He always wins who finds things amusing,
Despite the times when really he's losing.

Wit
Wit needs thought and a lively mind
With a whit of humour combined.

Word Choice
Indecency's words are rather obscene:
Decency wishes it knows what they mean.

Writers' Block
I can only hope I avoid writers' block;
If not, it would give me one hell of a shock.

Writers' Circle
With no start, no middle and no conclusion,
A writers' circle would end in confusion.

Writing Romances
What an intriguing business this is:
Years of effort for moments of bliss.

Yellow River
Crowding daffodils drowning the lawn
Seem to reveal how the Yangtze was born.

CHAPTER 25 with 22 two-liners

INFO TECH

App Number One
I remember the day in twenty-eleven,
When gadgeteers took us an app nearer heaven.

Computers
Computers induce higher levels of stress
Than those to which makers would wish to confess.

Emails
Daily occurrence confirmed her belief:
The fewer the emails, the less the grief.

Facts on Tap
Much knowledge is ready for instant use;
For the rest, the Net removes our excuse.

Faultless Faces
But for computers, we mightn't have seen
Those faultless faces in each magazine.

Games
Electronic games have changed the way
The brains of the young engage in play.

Google
The World Wide Web, with Google to boot,
Greatly eases one's info pursuit.

Identification
We have to have PINs, IDs and passwords, at least.
The police just wear numbers for keeping the peace.

Increasing Information
Increasing sources of information
Stretch our knowledge in every direction.

iPhone Men
In time gone by men have leant on their spade,
Now they belong to the iphone brigade.

IT Support
For IT support the old, of a sudden,
To family youth are wholly beholden.

Mobile Control
In view of such trouble as youngsters devise,
Control of their mobiles might sometimes be wise.

Phoning and Texting
Unceasing phoning and Internet texting
Removes all risk of one's ever forgetting.

Quiescence
A minute mitigation of noise that annoys
Is the silent technology texting employs.

Santa Line
Email's becoming the method of choice:
Next they'll be wanting their contact by voice.

Silicon Wafers
With microchips and semiconductors
Came non-metallic silicon wafers.

Social Digestion
This is the era of social digestion
That swallows the fodder of information.

Social Networking
Wide social networking's sure to expand,
New apps sustaining a constant demand.

Solar Light
When mock robin has charged his solar light,
He'll glow sublimely throughout the night.

Telephone
Installing a phone with a lousy guide
Turns out to be a matter of pride.

Too Tiny
Too tiny technology
Risks early futility.

Vanished Silence
A clacking of tongues and rattling of keys
Alas, are the modern library's disease.

CHAPTER 26 with 74 two-liners

LANGUAGE

Advancing Language
'Omigod' shows how language advances,
Combining words to suit our own fancies.

Aitch Appeal
The lower classes have known for ages
Elevation means sounding your aitches.

Alien Dilemma
Discovering life during space exploration
We'd face the dilemma of language translation.

Aphorisms
Aphorisms, concise and witty,
Sometimes embody hints of pity.

Architection
As old buildings drift into dereliction,
We could do with new words like architection.

Bores
Those who say draw-ring for drawing
Discerning listeners find boring.

Ciphers
Words have meaning, minds have thoughts;
Ciphered wording thinking thwarts.

Clarity
Clarity's key in achieving your aim,
Rehearse with care what you need to explain.

Clichés
Old clichés play a welcome role
Letting one feel they're in control.

Clicking at Ease
A constant clicking of alphabet keys
Hints that the writer is well at ease.

Conference Pears
The source of their name, you'll surely discover,
Is where delegates blether one with each other.

Connotations
'Promiscuous' chimes with indiscriminate;
As do 'casual', 'many' and 'intimate'.

Contextual Protest
Taking quotations way out of context
May generate a measure of protest.

Diphthong
Whenever two vowels merge into one,
The life of a diphthong has just begun.

Double Negatives
Where anything isn't without an opposite,
Two negatives ably create a positive.

Early Words
When whistles and grunts begat nouns and verbs,
Women began their obsession with words.

Earth's Surface
A recent intrusion one has to deplore
Is footballers calling Earth's surface the floor.

Eloquence
Oratorical pros are allowed to orate,
Whereas eloquent speakers may not eloquate.

English
By so many routes our language came,
And increasingly it spreads its fame.

Expression
Transporting great thoughts to meaningful speech
Is sometimes too far for brain cells to reach.

Fact-finding
When fumbling for facts during conversation,
We're often in debt to imagination.

Fewer or Less
To number-reductions 'fewer' applies,
While 'less' does the same for strength, weight and size.

First Thoughts
'What I meant to say' is a second beginning.
She wasted the first: she hadn't been thinking.

First Words
The very first words that come to mind
Beat all others we struggle to find.

From Zed to Zee
We lent them our language to get them going,
And now it's the Yankee lingo that's growing.

Grammar
The laws of language impose their own power:
Even the monarch is governed by grammar.

Hadrian Accents
Up around Durham their accents get broader
As if to be warning the Scottish marauder.

Immutable Words
After words have touched the page or the tongue,
They can't be retrieved, whether right or wrong.

Impertinence
It's easy to see that impertinence
Brags a syllable more than impudence.

Improval
He found a new word that looked like improval;
Alas, the critics rebuffed its approval.

Kingdoms
Kings gave their eponymous name to the realm,
And it stays a kingdom with queens at the helm.

Language
As each way of sharing our thoughts confirms,
Language is more than the sum of its terms.

Latest Slang
The young, who came wordless into this land,
Keep parents abreast of the latest slang.

Latin and Greek
Latin and Greek had a distance to travel;
Small wonder they took a while to unravel.

Lexical Extras
The dictionary brags it knows every word,
Although it won't print a few that I've heard!

Lingo
Lacking our lingo, where would we be?
Swinging with monkeys from tree to tree.

Linguistics
Linguists attempt to refine our language;
Slovenly slang's their main disadvantage.

Mails
An email excuses poor syntax and spelling:
The impact with post mail is always more telling.

Maxim and Axiom
A maxim and an axiom
Just miss each other's anagram.

Meaning Scheming
Ambiguity keeps the reader alert:
A first meaning might to another convert.

Monologues
A monologue's simply a one-way version
Of omnidirectional common conversing.

Mother Tongue
A people's language, much more than its land,
Is the pillar on which all nations stand.

Motormouth
A motormouth isn't only loquacious,
His speed of speaking is simply outrageous.

Not Knowing
To say 'I'm not sure' lets ignorance show;
It's a euphemism for 'I don't know'.

Odd Saying
Among the funny things we say,
The quaintest one is 'Let's make hay'.

Out and Out
Saying 'out and out' sounds like mere repetition;
What it's come to mean is 'beyond competition'.

Palindrome
Each visit is quick for a palindrome:
No sooner it's left than it's right back home.

Pauses
When speeches are made, what causes applause is
Less probably words than tactical pauses.

Philology
Philologists study the structure of language:
How feisty terms flourish while lazy ones languish.

Phrases
The writer's delighted fine phrases abound,
Except when the best of them's not to be found.

Platitude
A wonderful phrase too frequently used
Becomes reduced to a mere platitude.

Proverbs
On the open seas of spoken language,
Proverbs provide a welcoming anchorage.

Pseudonym
A pseudonym isn't a name that was given,
It's a pen name for which a use has arisen.

Punctuation
With subtle touches of punctuation,
Writers reveal their edification.

Quotability
Adding the gist of a spicy quotation
Can give some flavour to stale conversation.

Quotations
Some noted remarks are astute or exciting,
While many quotations don't merit reciting.

Remaining Terms
Some terms remain as if chipped from stone,
Such as granny flat and nursing home.

Rhetoric
Rhetorical language won't let you digress:
Its intention is choosing words that impress.

Ricepaper
Why should linguists ignore good advice?
Ricepaper isn't produced from rice!

Same Again
Is there another word for synonym?
If not, let's dub it antiantonym.

Scribbling Words
Once you have found that appropriate word,
Scribble it down to recall what occurred.

Simplification
When detail degrades a speaker's intention,
The remedy lies in simplification.

Slang
When slang was more spoken that written down,
Its ancient usage had greater renown.

Speech
Fluency's part is articulation:
Eloquence adds its share of persuasion.

Speech Writers
Each writer of speeches is duly devoted
To finding words that aspire to be quoted.

Surfeit of Words
On top of the regular nouns and verbs,
An editor gleans a surfeit of words.

Thesaurus
When searching for words we need a thesaurus,
A useful assistant to have before us.

'Tis OK
A beneficial thief is *'tis:*
It steals the doubt from *it's* and *its.*

Unsure
Among some people I wish they'd abjure
Saying 'I think' when they mean 'I'm not sure'.

You Bet
'Maybe' quotes an even chance:
'Likely' might one's odds enhance.

Vocabulary
Old words we discard and new manufacture;
Our daily usage the ultimate master.

Wholly Spent
'Complete' and 'finished' are differently meant
When one means whole and the other means spent.

Words of Wisdom
There's wisdom in words, but only in those
Which are both well chosen and well composed.

Words Unused
Words sometimes decide they don't want to be used,
Which results in some of us getting confused.

CHAPTER 27 with 31 two-liners

LAW

Anxiety
Passing anxious time when the jury is out,
A suspect swings on the pendulum of doubt.

By-laws
When stating non-enforced provisions,
By-laws yield to our own decisions.

Deadlock
When accepted experts' arguments fail,
No arbitration's of any avail.

Europe's New Statutes
While Europe's new statutes keep pouring in,
Those of old Britain might start to look thin.

Extradition
Extradition takes crooks who've dodged doing time
And shuttles them back to the scene of the crime.

Felons
Punishment follows the felon, not the crime:
It isn't the felony has to do time.

His Verdict
Lord X, the judge who went to the races,
Found it more fun than most of his cases.

Ignorance of the Law
Not knowing what certain parts of the law are
Is never excused - except for the lawyer!

In Balance
Perpetration of light-fingered crimes
Can easily lead to weighty fines.

Indecision
'On the one hand' or 'On the other' he'd waver,
Not telling the jury which hand he would favour.

Jurors
It isn't nice to be one of the jurors
When dressed up lawyers are sitting before us.

Justice
His Honour was wont to explain that justice
Was wisdom and truth together in practice.

Law
The doors of justice are closed on treason:
The walls of law are founded on reason.

Law Breaking
The saying that laws were made to be broken
Could many a criminal act betoken.

Lawless Fun
No statute's in force for protecting our fun,
Although on occasion our fun's overdone.

Laws of the Land
Every new statute our monarch endorses
Comprises clauses the rule-book enforces.

Legal Jargon
Though not comprehending its clauses galore,
There's no circumventing the wrath of the law.

Legal Procedures
After all in the court have been asked to rise,
There are legal procedures to exercise.

Legal Protection
Conviction under the rule of law is
Also a shield from fears of injustice.

Legalese
Till you've learnt to translate the language he uses,
Postpone the debate your attorney proposes.

Liberty
Liberty needs its strict limitations:
Criminals aren't allowed their intentions.

Loopholes
Laws seem like nets with unequal holes:
Large for the rich, the rest for poor souls.

No Warranty
A matter of fact isn't guaranteed truth:
It's simply a statement still seeking a proof.

Obligation
Be it through morals or litigation,
Nothing's more binding than obligation.

Precedents
Precedents tell us what went before;
Evidence lets us be doubly sure.

Public Opinion
While precedents dominate rulings in court,
Wise public opinion should always be sought.

Reportage
Fair comment is free, albeit offensive;
Libel, however, is always expensive.

Scales of Justice
Where threats displace the rule of law,
The scales of justice weigh no more.

Sobriety
Though it's axiomatic that judges are sober,
This mayn't be the case when presidings are over.

Tax Matters
Tax avoidance is deemed to be legal:
Its evasion, though, teeters on evil.

Tenets
Unprincipled people tend to ignore
The principal tenets of common law.

Verbal Contracts
Verbal contracts are simple to say,
Their actual sense so hard to convey.

CHAPTER 28 with 64 two-liners

LIFE

Careless
Nature expects that most women won't care
To protect their assets from men who dare.

Chances
Whoever we are, whether dolt or sage,
We're offered chances at life's every stage.

Clouds
Like clouds our lives share this perplexing trait:
Nor joy nor woe may we anticipate.

Contraception
Provided strict calendar-counts are obeyed,
Catholic ladies evade conception today.

Co-production
Those co-producers, husband and wife,
Are pleased to present their newborn life.

Copulation
Among earth's creatures, one only has found
An excuse to copulate all year round.

Daytime's Light
Once daytime's light has shrunk away,
We count the hours till brightening day.

Death
Acquiring our needs is one of life's battles;
Death is the entrance to life without chattels.

Don't Worry
Life may throw its problems at us:
Ultimately nothing matters.

Eating for Two
Food for the mother is food for her child,
Throughout the time of its growing inside.

Ersatz Nature
Fake flowers, lawns, and even trees?
Spare some space for life, if you please!

Fecundation
Cutting and grafting sustain the same breed;
Pairing and mating make new ones proceed.

Fortunate
Fortunate those who count patience their friend,
Allowing the tide of life to extend.

Future Presence
For life to ensure a future presence
The pairing of mates provides the essence.

Happy Families
Before TV and other diversions
Forebears counted their cousins in dozens.

Judgement
People, like plays, should never be rated
Until their last act has been enacted.

Life
Endeavour to fill the hours that slip by:
Life's more than just living until you die.

Life's Account
Your lifetime's account uses minutes and years;
Do not let their usage fall into arrears!

Life's Autumn
There's a time to progress and a time to retire,
But the season between is the one we desire.

Life's Cycle
June in the garden finds fledglings feeding:
June on the beach hears seniors wheezing.

Life's Endeavour
The mere achievement of ripe old age
Can life's endeavour never assuage.

Life's Episodes
Our living proceeds as episodes do,
Successively reaching new scenes to view.

Life's Evolution
It's unlikely science will find a solution
To plotting the future of life's evolution.

Life's Habits
We wear the habits of life at our choosing:
Improving, erring, revising, excusing.

Life's Journey
Our life is a journey to death from birth:
A proffered pursuit for proving our worth.

Life's Juncture
While paused at life's juncture, we've cause to discover
Historians go one way and prophets the other.

Life's Lessons
It takes manifold sessions
To unfold all life's lessons.

Life's Mysteries
Life's mysteries surround the world
Like static flags that hang unfurled.

Life's Pages
The pages of life create a great tome,
Recording past deeds for which we'll atone.

Life's Treasures
Remember life's treasures along the way:
The love you have kept and care to display.

Lifetime
Looking forward when young, your life lasts forever:
Looking later, however, it isn't that clever.

Lifetimes
Each soul departs for its destination
In thrall to mortal procrastination.

Living's Equilibrium
When one door closes as one is opened,
Living's balance is surely betokened.

Living's Riddle
Living's a riddle we have to address;
Much of its purpose we just have to guess.

Midlife Crisis
After forty-odd years, with us hardly knowing,
A disruption occurs that tests where we're going.

Mind Blowing
If one fine day you lie searching your mind,
You might be amazed by what you would find.

Mind Weeding
If I could weed my memory's bed,
I'd first reject the rubbish I've read.

Needing and Giving
Women like to believe they've got what men need:
Men likewise perceive they've to give to succeed.

Neverlasting
No matter how strong or apparently clever,
There's none on this earth can continue forever.

One-way Ticket
Since Nature gave us a one-way ticket,
Our test is finding how best to use it.

Only the Best
In life, as with music, we cherish the best
And with resignation put up with the rest.

Opportunity
If opportunity taps at your door,
Let him change the life that you lived before.

Optimism
See pleasure in trees; hear joy in a song;
Find goodness in people; life isn't long.

Pawns of Life
Midst races on earth where conflict is rife,
Children are pawns in the chess-match of life.

Pessimism
Life can be like what pessimists utter:
Just one damned thing that follows another.

Petals of Life
The petals of life all flourish in turn,
Then wither and perish, to our concern.

Photo Displays
Those photos displayed on one's mantelpiece
Reveal how quickly our birthdays increase.

Precautions
Precautions are taken when danger is high,
And likewise when risk of conception is nigh.

Pregnant Admission
'I've done it now!', the lady said;
She'll look well fed in months ahead.

Protection
Instantly after the act of conception,
The womb assumes its role of protection.

Pubertal Control
Pubertal partners test their control as
Surfers who tackle the swirling rollers.

Rapture
Without the rapture of woman with man,
Life wouldn't have flourished since time began.

The Relay Race
Our living resembles a relay race:
We toil till another soul takes our place.

Repentance
When all the energy of living is spent,
There's one thing still remains, and that is repent.

Reproduction
Just pip and pollen, sperm and seed:
All that's needed to let things breed.

Secret Lives
Tossed on the waters of joy and strife,
Each of us harbours a secret life.

Seduction
Successful seduction endorses the plan
That woman's conception is seeded by man.

Semen
When semen deposits an active sperm,
It hopefully yields a healthy return.

Sex
Sex dispenses enough motivation
To guarantee sufficient conception.

Sex Success
In its myriad forms of expression,
Sex is the motor of all succession.

Silly Affair
With arguments here and arguments there,
Life sometimes seems such a silly affair.

Stages of Life
All mortals have stages that plot their lives,
Like the seedling that blossoms, fades and dies.

Taking Account
When the fund of your living comes to be spent,
Be certain there's little of which to repent.

The World Unfurled
Like leaves on a tree when neatly unfurled,
Each of us lives in our own little world.

CHAPTER 29 with 125 two-liners

LIFESTYLE

Adventure
Without adventure, life isn't complete;
Domestic living's one's easy retreat.

Auto Suggestion
Just on its looks they choose their new car;
This tells us lots about who they are.

Aversion
The least suggestion of DIY
Provokes his usual question, 'Why?'.

B&B Visitors
Some visitors find a way they can see
To treat your nice house like a B&B.

Bachelorhood
A bachelor, once an unwedded man,
Disclaims that name when a partner's to hand.

Best Guests
With new carpets fitted, the guests they'll choose
Are bound to be those who remove their shoes.

Bidets
Designed for both anal and genital places,
Bidets help you wash the most awkward of spaces.

Bikinis
When brief bikinis became all the rage,
They showed us the start of a brand new age.

Black Tie
It's strange 'black tie' means men's evening wear:
Alone it's only a meagre affair.

Chocolate Box Fixers
When a chocolate box holds pins and glue
It shows that women can fix things, too.

Concealment
What cosmetics conceal
Is of little appeal.

Conspicuous Consumption
If you over-consume and cause a fuss,
Your excesses should be conspicuous.

Cosmetics
Albeit cosmetics can reassure,
They're purely a remedy, not a cure.

Cutting Corners
Those who cut the corners of living
Might find their journey's less forgiving.

Daughter
Each year he watches her blossom anew
And happily sees her children ensue.

Dishwasher
Those lucky enough to own a dishwasher
May think their kitchens can't get any posher.

Displacements
The old family hearths have been displaced
By TV screens of indifferent taste.

Domestic Automation
Domestic routines, throughout the nation,
Are bound to succumb to automation.

Domestic Success
A wife, two kids, three dogs, four pairs of green wellies
Convey - to a man - what domestic success is.

Don't Rush
Don't rush the jobs you have in store,
Improvements are worth waiting for.

Earlier Passions
Pray we return to earlier passions;
Today life's centred on chefs and fashions.

Egocentric Lady
Slighting whatever around her occurs,
She's in command of her own universe.

Elegance
Elegance values the help of deportment,
Deeming good posture of special importance.

Empty Houses
Where nobody sleeps or answers the phone,
Our empty houses are never a home.

Energetic Exercise
Energetic exercise
Gives you bright and sparkling eyes.

Enticement
Cool elegance chooses to strut its stuff,
While fragrance suggests its scents do enough.

Escapes
From gnawing chores on tedious days
We make our escapes in various ways.

Etiquette
When 'Dear Mr Pemberton' switched to 'Hi John',
He realized courtesy's manners had gone.

Family Ties
The ties of family bind the knot
Modern society nearly forgot.

Feeling the Breeze
To feel the breeze caress her breasts,
She has to risk the peeping pests.

Fixed Ways
Become a person who's fixed in their ways:
The consequent saving on effort repays.

Flippancy
Those adorably vacuous bling-bling dames
Ostentatiously play their socialite games.

Freeloader
Once a freeloader's learned his vocation,
That's your last trip to reciprocation.

Fuel Fools
Modern mankind shows people to be
Fools who use fuels as if they were free.

Giving
It isn't the value of what we give,
In the end it tells us the way we live.

Gossiping
Though sometimes slipping to impropriety,
Gossip's the oil of modern society.

Growing Grief
When the wealthy keep adding bits and pieces,
It's no wonder their neighbours' grief increases.

Habit
You can toss an old jacket over your shoulder
Until a new habit decides to take over.

Habits
Habits are something you don't have to buy,
You simply acquire them as time slips by.

Hats
Hats, mainly meant to attract or defend us,
Can range from the stupid to quite stupendous.

Her Gown
Her gown suggests a fulsome spinnaker
Billowing handsomely out before her.

High Ideas
She decorates her face for nigh an hour,
Blonde hair piled high as the Eiffel Tower.

Hot Chicks
In case your dictionary's raised a doubt,
Hot chicks are birds who like to chill out.

Hot Chocolate
When she's completed her stint at the sink,
She always enjoys a chocolate drink.

House Hunting
When choosing a house, the first items to check
Are the kinds and number of neighbouring pets.

House Proud
Your house wears a smile with visitors due:
The jobs on its list will now be rushed through.

Irritations
Wherever it is that you choose to reside,
You'll find irritations you just can't abide.

Jewel Box
Pity the jewel, exquisitely crafted,
Living its days in a hidden casket.

Just Us
The more in the house, the less you agree:
Harmony reigns when it's just you and me.

Kettle
A boiling kettle that bubbles its song
Invites the morning to sputter along.

Lavender
The lavender sachet her ladyship keeps
Lies under her pillow, ensuring she sleeps.

Lever Savers
An aggregate waste of water is stopped
By taps with levers in lieu of screw-topped.

Life's Variety
Releasing our minds from narrow anxiety
Frees us to savour life's wider variety.

Lifestyle Change
Among shifts in lifestyle, one's quite explicit:
The sleepover's overtaken the visit.

Majesty
One could tell by the carriage's extra gilt livery,
The lady inside was a special delivery.

Manicure
Trimming your nails, both fingers and toes,
Satisfies more than you might suppose.

Mariner Moll
The captain's table was not her intention:
The Sailor's Arms her preferred destination.

Mobile Libraries
For folk who rely on mobile libraries,
It's doubly important to check their diaries.

Mobile Phones
Everyday life in so many homes
Is now dependent on mobile phones.

Mock Tudor
Today's Tudor dwelling is quaintly deceiving
With loft insulation and under-floor heating.

Moderation
The less we possess, the more we treasure;
In modesty's dress we find most pleasure.

Modernity
Prone to project like the tail of a pheasant,
Modernity probes outside of the present.

Mores
When families disperse as modern ways require,
Our social rites reverse and kinship-bonds expire.

Mothers
Mothers are glad to be thought as
Their own delectable daughters.

Mothers Matter
No matter what other opinions we've heard,
In fact it's the mothers who manage the world.

Moving In
If you've bought an old mansion and just moved in,
It must be quite hard knowing where to begin.

Must Have
Must have, must have! No, there's no need!
Refrain from concessions to greed!

New Spouse
Not long since a bachelor, now a spouse,
He'll need to enhance his DIY nous.

Niches
The reason you place each vase in a niche
Is to keep it safely, well out of reach.

No Charge
When visitors come, they act as at home:
Each seeks a socket for feeding their phone.

Odorous Choice
Natural perfume bodes procreation:
Scent from a bottle begs recreation.

Ostentation
When ladies go dining to show off their rings,
They're mainly the choicest of granny's old things.

Out of Town
They gab as they walk, and with eyes on the ground
They miss the delights that around them abound.

Participation
What matters in life is participation;
Little profit accrues from isolation.

Parties
Parties are fun when you know everyone;
Excepting that case, they test your aplomb.

Patches and Darns
Our new patches and darns appear evidential
Of someone at hand who's distinctly prudential.

Peachy Looks
Young ladies aspire to a peachy complexion,
Applying cosmetics, evading detection.

Person of Habit
It pays to become a person of habit:
Savings on effort ensure a profit.

Plant Aid
Your indoor plants need constant care,
The problem comes when you're not there.

Pleasure
We'll sometimes regret the jobs we take on,
Then feel really pleased when they've been well done.

Pleasure Seeking
A problem confronting the pleasure seeker
Is that his assets get weaker and weaker.

Preparations
Those off the cuff preparations we make
Can often turn out to be a mistake.

Proclivity
People who share a certain proclivity
Adhere to a constant regularity.

Quizzes
Throughout the numerous quizzes today,
Knowledge is used in a purposeless way.

Residences
A residence is where a family resides,
Though at times it serves as a showpiece besides.

Rich Obligation
It appears the plutocrat's one obligation
Is living by others of similar station.

Role Models
The roles that role models often pursue
Can turn out to have the likeness of you.

Routines
Living tends to decline into daily routines:
The older you get, the fewer that means.

Scented Lady
The scented garden casts its own spell;
A fragranced lady aims to as well.

Screen Sense
Limit your leisure time facing a screen:
The wasted living you'll never redeem.

Scuppered Supper
His darling wife, devourer of pages,
Hasn't, he says, cooked supper for ages.

Segregation
Girlfriends are one thing and wives another:
They segregate into playmate and mother.

Shaving
A man with a razor may choose to begin
By shaving the stubble that's grown on his chin.

Shopaholics
Shopaholics give birth to 'must-have' children
Who later acquire that adult addiction.

Single Fingers
It takes a good towel to get one's hands dry
By making each finger singly comply.

Sloth
To those who live a life of pleasure,
Sloth means nothing else but leisure.

Sloth and Drinking
Sloth and drinking too much beer
Make folk turn distinctly queer.

Small Tags
Small tags attached in various garments
Start you itching in tender departments.

Smiler
Fix a meal then iron the pile:
Gratefully savour baby's smile!

Snobs
Snobs look down their noses at plebs,
Even at those who pose as celebs.

Social Occasions
What social occasions quaintly demand
Is standing around, a glass in the hand.

Socialites
They scan the pages for faces they know,
And when they find them invectives let go.

Squandering Life
Spending one's time where drug-taking's rife
Is how to squander the assets of life.

Stags and Hens
The stag party thrives on strippers and beers,
While ladies mix wine with sighs and oh dears.

Stormy Times
Through the stormier times of living,
Families ought to be more forgiving.

Street Walking
Parading her wares she catches his eye.
The randy man stares at what he might try.

Success
They display success, young men and their mates,
On motor car badges and number plates.

Sunrooms
Attractive to spiders and faded old chairs,
Some sunrooms may rate as mixed-blessing affairs.

Swim
The lady takes a daily swim
To keep her supple bits in trim.

Take a Break
Information, data, statistics, facts!
Dear Lord, pray spare us an hour to relax.

Tarantella
Active ladies like dancing the tarantella:
It favours a dress like a whirling umbrella.

Tasteless Days
When days are tasteless and stimuli lack,
Variety brings life's flavours right back.

Their Children
No one could shout their message much louder:
Of their two children they couldn't be prouder.

Tiffs
Putting all your domestic tiffs to rights
Is bound to precipitate restless nights.

Time to Shop
Life's hectic pace leaves so little time
Some shun the shops and purchase online.

Tint-and-Trim
If somebody needs to be impressed,
Just a simple tint-and-trim is best.

Turn-ups
Though at the time they might have looked funny,
Turn-ups on trousers could catch dropped money.

Upper Class
Among the untutored, some surmise
That upper class means terribly wise.

Vacuum Performers
Your ultimate choice of vacuum performers
Should take account of your furniture's corners.

Vanity
They think we've nothing better to do
Than fix our hair with lacquer and glue.

Visitor Tension
On every occasion when visitors come
We're tense lest there are things we ought to have done.

Visitors
Visitors sometimes denote their leaving,
Hoping no doubt to restart their eating.

Waterproof
At classy repasts where toffs are clustered,
Glasses of water don't cut the mustard.

Work and Play
Balancing hours of work and play
Always seems weighted worktime's way.

Yoga
Strenuous sessions of multi-tasking
Call on yoga for pressure-relaxing.

CHAPTER 30 with 36 two-liners

LITERATURE

All in the Mind
Immersed in a novel, you'll certainly find
You're lost in the world of another one's mind.

Authors
Most books are written with readers in mind;
Variants are those to vainglory inclined.

Authorship
Reading reviews of their filial book,
Authors reflect on the effort it took.

Autobiography
If you want to record what you undertook,
There's no better way than to write your own book.

Best-sellers
Best-sellers wear ravishing quotes on their jackets
Before the poor book-sellers open their packets.

Book Makers
Books we've learnt most from have seldom made riches
For scholarly publishers or their printers.

Books
The choosing of books is like browsing a menu:
Whatever your preference, there's something to rouse you.

Books on Shelves
A future moment will surely arrive
When books on shelves will no longer survive.

Books Overlooked
The enchantment of books in old inglenooks
Can be something a makeover overlooks.

Choosing Books
When perusing non-fiction for items to pick,
Reading useful subtitles won't take you a tick.

Classics
The classics, gems of two ancient nations,
Are famous for their many quotations.

Copyright ©
A proverb displaying a 'c' in a circle
Might conceivably seem a tad controversial.

Dear Aunty
Many thanks for the parcel and care that you took,
But I already have a very nice book.

Digital Literature
It looks as though publishing's set to dwindle
Now most of our books are destined for Kindle.

Experiential Nourishment
Where experience nourishes
Good literature flourishes.

Fiction Writer
A writer of fiction, he found himself driven
To fashion new lives from the hints he'd been given.

Followers of Fiction
Leda, per Zeus, had quads to succeed her;
Hence the game came of follow-my-leader.

Ghost Writing
Autobiographies often rely
Much less on selves than their titles imply.

Good Books
A good book is a tutor, friend and pleasure,
A stimulation to greater endeavour.

Impressive Classics
Classics persistently occupy shelves,
Silently looking impressed with themselves.

Latest Book
Recalling the latest book that she read,
It's ten to one she'd been nestling in bed.

Lit Crit
The treatise on literary criticism
Should easily be the finest book written.

Lost Silence
Disruptive chatter and rattling of keys
Of late have become the library's disease.

Mistakings
The quoting of wordings known writers have penned
Lends subsequent authors a risk to forfend.

Nomenclature
On books of fiction the author's writ large;
For serious works the title's in charge.

Nonsensical Writing
Alas some authors still seem to abstain
From making the sense of their writing plain.

Not a Jot
There's no jotting a line with that blight, writer's block;
It's like telling the time when you haven't a clock!

Old Library
They watched the old library disappear,
Replaced by a venue for snacks and beer.

Opting Out
She feared she'd misspelt a word in her book,
But for peace of mind opted not to look.

Reading
The best of reading is meeting, refreshed,
One's corpus of knowledge already possessed.

Reviewers
They'll criticize what they mayn't comprehend,
And risk a reprisal they can't defend.

Reviews
Authors whose fortune depends on reviews
Will laud their critics or hurl them abuse.

Sources
Books, once seen as the true university,
Now admit sources of greater diversity.

Worthy Words
Although his works are old and few,
The words he wrote ring fresh and true.

Writers
Writers aren't wise in being predictive;
Fame is safeguarded by being suggestive.

Writing
Writing's unlikely to sound commercial
Without some content that's controversial.

CHAPTER 31 with 148 two-liners

LOVE & MARRIAGE

Adoration
Love is the target of adoration,
A certain route to multiplication.

Adultery
Extramarital partners choose to cohabit;
Adultery's more a discretionary practice.

Adventitious Romance
An adventitious circumstance
Can spark the fire of true romance.

Affairs
Designs of the extramarital kind
Are detected by signs that slip the mind.

Affection
Opening sex to closer inspection
Disposes courters to greater affection.

Afters
When a chap says the evening is all inclusive,
His hinting at afters is highly conducive.

Allure
There's many a quarry has parried a lure;
Allure in a woman is there to make sure.

Allurement
When girlhood all its allurement deploys,
The incentive comes for boys to be boys.

Amorous Aims
Most amorous aims are likely to fail
Despite the scheming they're prone to entail.

Amorous Consequences
A pair intent on their intimate sessions
Don't care to dwell on their consequent lessons.

Askings
Albeit they're prone to end in refusals,
The lady still likes to receive proposals.

Attachment
Getting attached to each other is fun,
Unlike the time when the knot comes undone.

Bearded Affection
While some bearded men are craving attention,
Attentive ladies seek bearded affection.

Bigamist
To choose between them he clearly was loath,
So in the end he decided on both.

Blushing
Other than lovers who've taken to blushing
Know the direction in which they've been pushing.

Bonding
What is it bonds young lovers together?
A trace of chemistry laced with pleasure.

Bright Eyes
Bright eyes alight with burning desire,
Ignite your mate with similar fire!

Burgeoning Bosoms
Her burgeoning bosoms kept lovers at bay,
Except for the others who liked them that way.

Candles
Once, wax and wick both cheated the night;
Now they promise romantic delight.

Checks and Balances
Those who achieve the happiest marriages
Clearly succeed with their checks and balances.

Condensation
Some condensation on cars' window panes
The breath of lovers discreetly explains.

Consequence
He'd observed that the waitress was scantily dressed;
With the tip she received she was greatly impressed.

Contact
That instant in time when your eyes met mine
Was surely inspired by a source divine.

Cool Prude
Though rudimentary, love might intrude
Upon the cool of a sensitive prude.

Coupling
Couples are part of the magic of love:
They match up together like hand and glove.

Creation
Insistence, Resistance, Persistence.
Acceptance, Endurance, Emergence.

Credit for Love
Those who've discovered contentment in love
Should give due credit to Cupid above.

Dating
Awaiting a date, checking all things vital,
Cosmetics ensure the lady's not idle.

Dating and Lusting
Dating's the game of evaluation;
Lusting's the engine of procreation.

Deceiving
No fancy words completely recover
The state before deceiving one's lover.

Demure
It's seldom a lady of aspect demure
Will take second place in respect of allure.

Destitution
When they reach a state of destitution,
Women might slip into prostitution.

Divorcing
Couples tend to spend more time in their courting
Than ever's done in the course of divorcing.

Doormat
His wife's like a doormat that's curled on the floor:
She'll watch as he trips on the lies he forswore.

Dormant Desire
Amorous passion lies dormant within,
Yearning for meetings when stirrings begin.

Eagerness
The look of love imbues her eyes
With eagerness she can't disguise.

Enticing Eyes
When eyelashes lower and slyly rise,
He's held by the spell of enticing eyes.

Erogenous Brain
Media invasion of sex in the home
Has made the brain an erogenous zone.

Extra Attraction
A modicum of indiscretion
Lends a lady extra attraction.

Extra Time
Arrived at an impasse they couldn't define,
They agreed on a session of extra time.

Fancied Woman
Whatever emotion she tries to disguise,
A woman who's fancied has stars in her eyes.

Female Perception
Perceptive women discovered one day
They might want to love, but needn't obey.

Feminine Virtue
Virtue in women is man's presumption:
His later regret, his former compunction.

Fidelity
Fidelity plays a marital role,
Preventing distractions taking control.

Finest Time
It's the finest time of one's mortal span
When man loves woman, and woman loves man.

First Encounter
Their first encounter was tender, if brief:
A moment of rapture, beyond belief.

First Kiss
They sought that gift sublime, the moment they first kissed;
Within the book of time, their imprint must exist.

Flimsies
You could tell by the flimsies in which she was clad,
She was never as happy as when she was bad.

The Food of Love
Try the recipe, take a chance!
Love is the food of true romance.

Gentlemen
A gent who's adopted a highbrow taste
Will not approach ladies with undue haste.

Girls
Incremental advances
Can tickle girls' fancies.

Grudges
Reluctant to part, it's for parents to judge
If the flip side of love might just be a grudge.

Her Skirt
Her slim black skirt's an instant reminder
Of flirting years and inches behind her.

Hesitance
Love is a worry to hesitant men:
They know what they want, but can't decide when.

Homely and Kindly
A homely face and a kindly manner
Often bring man and woman together.

Hooker
A hooker takes exercise walking the streets,
Extending the circle of people she meets.

Hunkering Down
Replacing courtship's clamorous strife
Comes hunkering down as man and wife.

Husbands
Husbands can suffer the reputation
Of some slight lacking in dedication.

Husbands as Prey
When the man of the house is tempted to stray,
Other people's husbands are treated as prey.

Illicit Delight
Like a nightly moth that's attracted to light,
She's under the spell of illicit delight.

Imagining
When man's desires don't attain actuality,
Imagination replaces reality.

Imperfections
Partners concerned about imperfections
Shouldn't exaggerate expectations.

Impetuosity
Time should restrain the impetuous lover:
The pendulum's swinging ought to be slower.

Improbability
Impossibility ends a romance;
Improbability lends it a chance.

Infatuation
Infatuation brings couples together;
Dissatisfaction will part them, however.

Insomnia
The best antidote to insomnia, they say,
Is sleeping with someone you don't have to pay.

Inspections
Women inspect every male in the room
And try to detect which mate's with which groom.

Intimate Acts
She found, with delight, that intimates acts
Were brilliant ways to help her relax.

Jack and Jill
O, how they lied on the night they were wed:
He picturing Beth, she dreaming of Ted.

Jealousy
Mainly, the jealous may wish to prevent
A love affair with creative intent.

Jilted
Unfortunate men who find themselves jilted
Might find it's because their vigour has wilted.

Kept Woman
His discretionary woman, discreetly kept,
At dodging the neighbours was deftly adept.

Kissing
Youth soon learns the art of prolific kissing:
Old age turns the part to sweet reminiscing.

Ladies' Wants
It's hard to predict what a lady wants,
Except to reject the prigs she confronts.

Lady Who
The gamekeeper's clothes were grubby and creased
Before Her Ladyship's pony rides ceased.

Lasting Beauty
Once procured by discerning eyes,
Beauty endures in grateful minds.

Lookers and Seekers
There's more to a woman than looks alone,
And more than a man would like to be shown.

Love
In every facet of which it's possessed,
Love is the passion that heads all the rest.

Love and Logic
While led into logic fairly and squarely,
Men are lulled into loving unawarely.

Love and Marriage
True love's a balance with equal weights
And marriage a truce where neither dictates.

Love Chant
As she chants 'He loves me, he loves me not',
She feels that sheer chance is part of the plot.

Love's Endorsement
Every wedding ring roundly endorses
That love is the king of nature's forces.

Love's Equation
Forget subtraction and multiplication,
Falling in love is the neatest equation.

Love's Evocation
Among emotions in which we're engrossed,
Constantly love evokes memories most.

Love's Menu
Every emotion can offer a menu;
Love's is lust, care, and affection to tempt you.

Love's Poetic Limit
A popular topic, love's hard to harness:
It faces a limit on rhyming partners.

Love's Potion
They can say it's crazy or deem it weird,
Love is the potion that's mostly revered.

Love's Progress
The fumbling phase of loving's beginnings
In time's refined to subtler insistings.

Love's Resolve
As constellations must resolve,
Love flourishes on firm resolve.

Lovers
When lovers are bathed in evening's glow,
They'll impart their wish of new life to sow.

Lovers Beware!
Beware the lovelight in their eyes:
Love is more than lust implies.

Lovers' Words
Young lovers' words are lightly spoken,
Far deeper vows they likely betoken.

Loving's Emotion
Love is the summit of living's emotion;
Let us submit to it with our devotion.

Loving's Reversal
There once was a time when marriage came first,
But now love's sequence is often reversed.

Lying Lovers
The rule of law may not apply
When lovers with each other lie.

Madams
Power discounting accountability
Favours ladies of lesser gentility.

Marital Perfection
The perfect wife is what others might think
Until they see hubby stuck at the sink.

Marital Prowess
Not an adventure intended for cowards,
Marriage needs adequate marital prowess.

Marital Spats
Sometimes domestic disputes get involved;
Bedtime's when many such spats are resolved.

Marriage
Families gather when people get married:
A totem of permanence often disparaged.

Marriage Criteria
On the list of most men's criteria
I warrant you'll find a shapely posterior.

Matrimony
Matrimonial joys can hardly last
If one of the parties harks to the past.

Maturing Love
Self-love considers its own comfort first,
Until in real love it becomes immersed.

Mind and Manner
To norms of beauty she needn't conform:
They all enthral when the curtains are drawn.

Missed Kiss
The lady refrained from placing a kiss
In case her emotion ignited his.

Mistresses
Most young gentlemen learning life's mysteries
Ask if young ladies yearn to be mistresses.

Modern Cupid
When a beautiful woman shot him a glance,
It just could have led to a shotgun romance.

Name Disdain
She married a man then discarded his name,
Which in cricket is called not playing the game.

Needing and Giving
Women like to believe they've got what men need:
Men likewise perceive they've to give to succeed.

New View
A view of Victorian ankle was porn;
Today's full-on nudity launches a yawn.

Newly-weds
Self-satisfaction on newly-weds' faces
Won't augur well for marriage's embraces.

Nicely Designed
If men are to have designs on a lady,
She must have been nicely designed already.

No Return
Their marriage became of greatest concern
When both passed the insult of no return.

Pampering
Young lady lovers like to feel pampered;
Lacking the means, young swains feel hampered.

Power-dresser
Donning her slick black suit and tapered heels
She, power-dressed, to her quarries appeals.

Presence
If absence makes the heart grow fonder,
Presence must make it beat the stronger.

Private Affair
Though they tried to keep it a private affair,
Papers soon discovered the lovers' new lair.

Promiscuity
Not content with now, but looking ahead,
Promiscuous ladies keep open bed.

Pubescents
Pubescents who procrastinate
Submerge the urge to find a mate.

Puppy Love
Puppy love, we all learn,
Though intense, is short-term.

Romance's Stance
When fellows adopt a particular stance
Most ladies can tell that they're up to romance.

Rosy
It seems that no man could offer resistance
Once Rosy approached into touching distance.

Rosy Future
Bring me a bottle of rosy wine
And the rosy girl will soon be mine.

Saucy Caution
A saucy attraction may make one bolder,
Though not when caution looks over one's shoulder.

Schemer
Extremely attractive, though level-headed,
She'd wed old beans with a need to be steadied.

Second Chance
That first romance was to last her life through;
Her next best chance was as wife number two.

September Weddings
While April invokes her sweet yearnings ahead,
September's the month when most lovers are wed.

Sighs
Of all the signs of despair that exist,
Love's sighs must bide at the top of the list.

Something Afoot
When a wife agrees with her husband, beware!
There's something afoot, of which *he's* unaware.

Soonest
She lay in his arms soon after he'd met her;
Today they're to wed, the sooner the better.

Sparkle and Spice
What better brings sparkle and spice to life
Than couples becoming husband and wife?

Star Turns
As constellations must revolve,
Love flourishes on firm resolve.

Substitutions
After reviews of young beauties he tried,
A few substitutions led to a bride.

Suitors
Formerly she'd have been found a suitor:
Latterly finds her suitably cuter.

Summer of Love
Succeeding spring, when lusting is rife,
Love is the summer of human life.

Taken for Granted
He found out too late she'd suddenly departed:
He'd made the mistake of taking her for granted.

Teen Romance
In the tentative stage of teen romance,
Predictability hasn't a chance.

Tempting
Women who dress to tempt men to come running
Ought to know best what might be forthcoming.

Tootsie
Tootsie's a game for incipient lovers,
A tactile trick that each gender discovers.

Tug of Love
In loving's mighty tug of war
Pray stake a claim love can't ignore.

Valentine
This was our wish, and we know it came true.
You still love me, and I'm still loving you.

Volatile Vows
Sad volatile vows degenerate
Through alimony's legal debate.

Wedding
The courting overture felt like magic;
Now is the moment to face the music.

Wily Lady
She knew where to get the best of the action
Then rest when she'd had her ration of passion.

Women
Some are perceived as professional lovers;
Most others conceive as amateur mothers.

Women's Confession
Most women confess to having their say
And love to ensure that they get their way.

Young Love
Why young lovers walk hand in hand,
All who have loved will understand.

Young Lovers
Fill in space, then block out time,
And let young lovers entwine.

CHAPTER 32 with 38 two-liners

MEDIA

Another Chance
Repeating that film, to the programmer's credit,
Reminds you again that you won't want to watch it.

Appearance
When somebody knows they'll appear on TV,
It's a bet that they'll dress as smart as can be.

Auntie
Whatever became of the BBC?
It fell for the charms of fancy IT.

Boring Trawling
Much of telly is patently boring,
Mostly stemming from archival trawling.

Comedic Turns
Comedic shows once favoured hilarity;
Mainly now they're a show of vulgarity.

Copy Columns
Often known as copy, the words in a paper
In edited columns are cobbled together.

Costsavers
Assembled from clips of out-take and in-keep,
Those pick-and-paste programmes are soulless though cheep!

Dr Who: Drama of the Week
Here tragically lies the defining scene
In the sad demise of the BBC.

Editing
The editing room is often a world
Wherein invectives are constantly hurled.

Elderly Evenings
Plodding through listings and dodging repeats,
We keep hoping for programmes shown as treats.

Episodes
If episode one didn't grab you at all,
It's seldom worth trying the next few withal.

Fixed Images
It used to be said no camera lied;
How wickedly pictures are now contrived!

Folly Lolly
He with a brain who turns to folly
Knows what idiots earn on telly.

Hacks
Who stoop to feed us weird items they write?
The hacks whose columns celebrities blight.

Headlines
Provocative headlines might tempt us to buy
A paper we'd otherwise tend to decry.

Landscape
Landscape or seascape will set you free
From staring, rapt, at glaring TV.

Media Freedom
Disdaining the media's rough mediation,
Whatever's exceptional claims exception.

Moving Times
Off the fruits of repeats decreasingly feeding,
Stars who've fed us real treats see heydays receding.

News
Media's expresses hurtle bad tidings;
Trains with good news stand static in sidings.

News Exclusive
Exclusive's a term that denotes what's unique,
Though it might admit to including a leak.

Newsless
Ignoring the news as much as you can,
You're less informed but a happier man.

Newspapers
Great papers maintaining their circulation
Sustain a discussion throughout the nation.

Newsworthy
They say when a man bites a dog it's news.
Let's hope the poor pooch said assailant sues.

Old News
Once, commentators strove by heart
To learn what laptops now impart.

Out of the Can
Hark the canned laughter on comedy shows:
If switched too abruptly, everyone knows!

Paper Crumbs
The tastier crumbs politicians let fall,
We pick up next day at the newspaper stall.

Phoney Laughter
Whether it's shortly before or more likely after,
Some programmes are ruined by phoney laughter.

Postbags
Letters to papers are differently seen;
For most, they're a valve for letting off steam.

Premonition
TV's now akin to a premonition:
Reviewing old days in high definition.

Programmers
Watch feckless programmers maunder on;
The best of television has gone.

Reality Shows
So many reality girls and guys
Appear as failures to most people's eyes.

Soaps
Imagine TV when all programmes are soaps;
The whole of the nation would turn into dopes.

Tabloids
He felt he could say without contradiction
That tabloids fulfilled his ration of fiction.

Telly Ads
They speak their adverts in silly flat voices,
Ensuring viewers don't take any notice.

Telly Regurgitation
A spate of telly regurgitation
Defines the state of an ailing nation.

TV Choices
Oldsters find limited choice on the screen:
Youngsters much more they've not previously seen.

TV Soccer
Televised soccer annoys the ladies:
They hope the players will vanish in Hades.

Wearisome
Endless repeats occurring on telly
Aren't just wearis*ome* but weari*many*.

CHAPTER 33 with 47 two-liners

MONEY MATTERS

Accounting
Accountancy's remit has several parts:
One rumoured to be the creative arts.

Bankers
Bankers still wear sharp suits and drive smart cars,
But at least no longer smoke big cigars.

Banks
Banks were where we would beg on our knees;
Now they've begun to use the word 'please'.

Bargain
A gentleman's agreement, struck at ease,
Avoids the expense of legality's fees.

Barter
The Stock Exchange holds no coins of gold:
No money, just numbers are bought and sold.

Beyond Riches
Especially in times of financial depressions,
The insatiable rich increase their possessions.

Cash Flow
A way of preventing a cash-flow problem
Is circumventing the credit-card option.

Classes
Upper, middle, and lower denote the classes,
So that the Chancellor knows where the brass is.

Credit
Stop credit expenditure, urges the pundit,
Unless your resources can credibly fund it.

Dirty Cheats
It seems without trying cheats glean their wealth
Like dust accumulates on a top shelf.

Enthusing
When questing for wealth leads men to enthuse,
It tends to loosen their hold on the truth.

Fate's Rules
Fate doesn't keep to logical rules:
Inherited wealth can fall to fools.

Financiers
With their fees and charges and crafty commissions,
Financiers show they have no inhibitions.

Flush
A fortunate person with money to spare
Might buy a replacement and shun a repair.

Funding
The greatest good for the largest number's
A great escape for all pressured funders.

Gains
Illicit gains are fittingly despised:
No fruits of true endeavour criticized.

Gambler
Like an anxious racehorse approaching a fence,
He worried that failure meant heavy expense.

Giving Oneself
It befits us not to trade on wealth:
Our prime concern is giving oneself!

Illicit Gains
Illicit gains are fittingly despised:
No fruits of true endeavour criticised.

Insurance
For loss or damage obtain compensation
Having previously paid for such protection.

Investing
I fear for the novice who dares to invest:
He parts with his assets then hopes for the best.

Investments
The answer to questions on risk you ask, is
Spread your investments in several baskets.

Making Money
They say when the sun shines you're making money,
So when the rain falls it can't be that funny.

Money
Like heavenly bodies in thrall to the sun,
The stardom of living is money, for some.

Money Matters
A pecuniary setback makes most people flinch,
A reaction that lasts while they're feeling the pinch.

Moneyed Means
Toffs' massive enhancements bemuse the poor
Whose minor improvements mean so much more.

Old Gifts
Let's lavish old gifts that we've stashed away
On needy people unable to pay.

Pound Savers
Sponsored occasions where ladies lose weight
Shed pounds from the cost of health for the state.

Precious Time
To say time is money's an odd equation.
When it's far more precious than wealth creation.

Price and Value
As price and value live miles apart,
To pair them up you have to be smart.

Price Reductions
As prices reduce, new versions appear;
Which means the latest is always too dear.

Priced Out
Each improvement to technical gadgets
Imposes pressure on modest budgets.

Reality Counts
The rrp is what they show:
Reality is less, we know.

Receipts
Always keep each receipt that you've received
Or else there's a risk of being deceived.

Recessions
Successive disruptive recessions
Equate to one lasting depression.

Refunding
If you need to retrieve a deposit you've paid,
It's your right to demand a redemption is made.

Richness
No matter how rich the wealthy might be,
They will differ little from you and me.

Savings
Small savings made on the daily shopping
Will set the affluent snidely scoffing.

Sensible Spending
True happiness thrives on little expense
When limited money's wisely dispensed.

Statements
Banks ensure your spending isn't too rash:
Their statements tell you the state of your cash.

Tax Tactics
When Brits work abroad, the vital fact is
They're making the move to flee our taxes.

Top Brass
Top brass in big firms will pay themselves well;
Too much, and workers might start to rebel.

Validation
On validated statements we'll always rely:
Unwarranted assumptions can too often lie.

Vested Interests
When investing for gain he greatly preferred
To have vested interests already conferred.

Wealth Matters
Wealth doesn't start where poverty finishes:
In between them, hope never diminishes.

Wealth Propagation
Among known methods of procreation,
Wealth has the knack of self-propagation.

Worries Controlled
His chosen defence, of the ostrich kind,
Prevented odd debts distressing his mind.

CHAPTER 34 with 28 two-liners

MUSIC

Background Music
When background music's excessively loud,
That TV programme should not be allowed.

Bawdy Songs
Bawdy old songs, more than present-day hits,
Enlivened our minds and sharpened our wits.

Can Thrill
It takes an ego as big as the planet
To thrill a big gig, a technician to can it!

Cellist
With thighs open wide, enclosing her cello,
She wickedly faced the Spanish torero.

Choristers
There's much to be said for a regular choir,
Including the pleasure they thereby acquire.

Classical Music
Classics follow the maestro's direction
Of tutored notes, all honed to perfection.

The Conductor
A music conductor waving his hands
Has always to turn his back on his fans.

Diva
Temperament doesn't befit the beginner;
That is postponed till she's known as a winner.

Dominant Theme
The dominant theme in a piece of music
May lead to the need of an analgesic.

Encore
Once played, some music remains in the brain,
Repeating its theme like a sweet refrain.

Favourite Pieces
She wouldn't admit to a knowledge of music,
Albeit she knew full well how to choose it.

Karaoke
Renditions of songs in karaoke
Are hardly serious, far more jokey.

Maestro
The maestro's endeavour is coaxing each player
To come in on time and to finish together.

A Maestro's Message
Keep coming to concerts; don't think of stopping.
Enjoy some great music between the coughing.

Muses
Music's inspired by one of the Muses;
The type's defined by which Muse one chooses.

Music
Musical art, like that of a painter,
Embraces shape and colour, though fainter.

Music and Art
Naught avails us comparing music and art:
No value accrues from the critics' remarks.

Music Presenter
Dear presenter, after you've had your say
Just start the music then please go away.

Musical Games
With bassos profundos and high sopranos,
Accompanists play on their grand pianos.

Musical Route
Music borrows our ears, and imparts
The sorrows and joys that touch our hearts.

Musical Therapy
Listening relaxed to most classical music
Is stated as fact to be therapeutic.

Musical Totem
Praised soloists' totem of fame is
Their way of distorting their faces.

New Music
New composers seek to be clever:
Mozart's aim was creating pleasure.

Pianists
Those difficult notes in various places
Make pianists pull hilarious faces.

Piano Music
Piano music that fails to please
One must agree is a waste of keys.

Replayings
Too many replayings of works we enjoy
Can turn into pieces that start to annoy.

Scant Reward
The composer, alas, is often ignored:
His name in the programme's his only reward.

Voicing
Instrumental music could never replace
Aspirational notes of the human race.

CHAPTER 35 with 23 two-liners

NATIONALITY

Accord
A trusted accord with neighbouring nations
Requires precautions against aberrations.

Annoying
Among the freedoms a nation's enjoying,
The one to reject is being annoying.

Capacity
Although good old England is always a pull,
The time may have come to declare the land full.

Charters
In England made, our charters stand
On principles they still command.

Civilization
A civilized people shares equal respect
And a common regard it can rightly expect.

Countries
Most countries are only nations by name:
Through invasion and rape they grew the same.

Diversity
That nations have differences people expect;
Within them diversity needs more respect.

Emblems
A nation's emblems cannot be ignored
When their implications have been abhorred.

England's Glory
If you trace the pages of England's story,
You'll find it's not always one of glory.

English Village
The English village, eternally loved,
By pressures unjust is being engulfed.

Great Britain
Great Britain's a nation that harks to its past,
And looks to a future where freedom will last.

Incitement
Crude taunting of races can lead to incitement.
The ultimate cost is a formal indictment.

Incomers
Their habits were learnt in a distant land,
At a different knee. So, please, understand.

Independence
From pundits in Brussels we're laden with laws
That most of the nation intensely abhors.

Integration
Problems resulting from immigration
Involve the solving of integration.

Nationalism
Xenophobes practise dislike to excess;
Chauvinists add to their common distress.

Nationhood
A nation's composed of layered invasions,
Each one imposing its own aspirations.

Nations
Allowing for failings, almost all nations
Happily boast of their loyal populations.

Reinstatement
Having overtaken a revolution,
More strength accrues to the rule of a nation.

Remonstrance
When the people incline to remonstration,
It's clearly the sign of a fretful nation.

Republics
Exempting dynastic family circles,
Republics abjure hereditary titles.

Subjugation
Freed from the yoke of another nation,
A country rebuilds its fortification.

Workers and Shirkers
Diligence of foreign workers
Puts to shame some native shirkers.

CHAPTER 36 with 206 two-liners

NIFTY LINES

Abuse
Hurling abuse
Serves no good use.

Advising
Advice isn't heeded
By those who don't need it.

Alarm Clock
An alarm clock is used
So you'll catch the first news.

All Alone
He stood all alone
Like a standing stone.

Amok
Incredible luck
Sends nutters amok.

Ardour
Desist from desire:
To ardour aspire.

Assumption
What's not forbidden
Assumes permission.

Attractive
To remain attractive
You need to keep active.

Bad Conscience
Minds are seldom relaxed
When their conscience is taxed.

Bats' Delight
Do bats seek their delight
In the darkness of night?

Belief
It's in moments of grief
People question belief.

Bizarreness
Most bizarre though it seems,
We appear in our dreams.

Blabbing
Foreknowledge denies
A pleasant surprise.

Black Midges
Where black midges attack
You'd do well to turn back.

Blogetry
Uploaded blogetry
Equals e-poetry.

Boiler Repairers
Repairers of boilers
Are mostly cold toilers.

Boozing Losers
When soccer teams lose,
Fans flock to the booze.

Bottle Novel
Your hot-water bottle
Lets you read a novel.

Brolly Folly
The ultimate folly
Is rain without brolly.

Cachet
The cachet that's sought
Can't always be bought.

Calls for Help
When help calls are needed,
Make sure that they're heeded.

Car Drivers
Drivers shouldn't assume
That they've got enough room.

Cats and Dogs
Why do cats miaow
While dogs don't know how?

Change
An obsession with change
Is the curse of our age.

Chimeras
To come's a chimera
That never gets nearer.

Circumnavigation
Circumnavigate Earth
And you'll ponder its worth.

Circus
When the circus leaves town,
Faces wear their old frown.

Cogency
Cogent cogitation
Lessens hesitation.

Collectors
Obsessive collectors
Might pass as investors.

Comedians
Comedians convert
Our frowns into mirth.

Commuters
Commuters disprove
Delays will improve.

Comparisons
There's nothing compares
Like rabbits and hares.

Concealment
What cosmetics conceal
Is of little appeal.

Concentrating
Intense concentration
Incites perspiration.

Confessions
Facial expressions
Reveal confessions.

Conspiring Eyes
What her lips admit
He'll surely permit.

Copies
Imitations confess
The inventor's success.

Cupid's Consent
All the places they went
Were with Cupid's consent.

A Cyclist's Requirement
A cyclist requires
Two punctureless tyres.

Cynics
They devise new ills
To warrant more pills.

Dads
Each dad with a daughter
Should stress what he's taught her.

Delicious Dish
A dish that's delicious
Might not be nutritious.

Desertion
Any lover who's left
Leaves another bereft.

Desires
What a person desires
Greater effort inspires.

Diaries
Perceive today's histories
As yesterday's diaries.

Discontent
Discontentments occur
When ambitions don't work.

Disrespect
We've come to expect
Wealth's lack of respect.

Drivers
Fine them for speeding,
Not simply exceeding.

Dullness
It's sad how dullness
Becomes infectious.

Dupe
She calls him honey
Then spends his money

Early Retirement
An early retirement's
The end of excitement.

Ecosystem
An ecosystem
Isn't a fiction.

Encouraging
True stories of courage
Are told to encourage.

Envy's Message
Envy soon tells us
Not to be jealous.

Erudition
A second edition
Confirms erudition.

Etymology
Etymology traces
A lexicon's basis.

Excelling
If you want to excel
Just do better than well.

Excuses
Strong reason defuses
Our feeble excuses.

Experience's Teaching
Experience taught us
That nobody's flawless.

Explorers
Intrepid explorers
Like crossing new borders.

Facial Disgrace
A person's disgrace
Can show in their face.

False Laughter
The laughter's not real
If the joke's revealed.

Farewells
Farewells, one discerns,
Beg welcome returns.

Feeling Alone
When using your phone
You don't feel alone.

Fictions
A liar's addiction
Is rooted in fiction.

Flies
What you can't deny
Is that flies can fly.

Fly Timing
Their flight denies
The timing of flies.

Forecasting
Forecasting what's to come,
Let the prophets be dumb.

Foreign Workers
They will weigh their concerns
Against wages they earn.

Forgiving
The key to living
Unlocks forgiving.

Free Verse
A series of lines
In varied designs.

Frustration
Resisting temptation's
A source of frustration.

Genealogy
You're on more family trees
Than you'd ever believe.

Going Wrong
It doesn't take long
For things to go wrong.

Good Lookers
All cats look nice
To friendly mice.

Great and Small
Heed all creatures on earth:
Each one has its own worth.

Guilt
Seeking forgiveness
Hints you're not guiltless.

Hardly Barely
Hardly the concrete dries;
Barely the bather dives.

Heartbeats
A new lifetime can't start
Without beats of the heart.

Hearts
Our brains are but tools:
It's the heart that rules.

Her Wealth
She counted her wealth
On the fingers of health.

High Esteem
To be held in esteem's
A vainglorious dream.

High Heels
The sight of high heels
Is one that appeals.

Hunger
For herbs and spices,
Hunger suffices.

Immodesty
Immodesty eschew!
Friendship favours the true.

Incanting
She was never averse
To incanting a curse.

Incredulity
The incredulous mind
Leaves believing behind.

Inebriation
Inebriation denies
What's in front of its eyes.

Ineptness
Inept manufacture
Can lead to disaster.

Infallible Flattery
Persistent flattery
Succeeds infallibly.

Insight
His value was insight,
With a tongue q.

Intentions
Your every intention
Should get full attention.

Interdependence
As knowledge needs language,
So language needs knowledge.

Intriguing Reading
When a book's intriguing
It's well worth the reading.

Intrusion
Intrusion assumes
A rude interruption.

Job List
Just thinking about it
Won't see it completed.

Joy
It isn't the laughter:
It's the smile thereafter.

Lace-ups
Lace-up shoes aren't much use
If their laces come loose.

Lap Dancer
What a dancer exposes
The higher her price is.

Leaks
A memo leaked
Is mischief-briefed.

Lies in Excess
A lie may be surplus
To hiding its purpose.

Linguistic Rules
The rules of language
Bend to its usage.

Lion Reliance
You're mad to rely on
A somnolent lion.

Live Life
Kick worry away:
Live life by the day.

Looking Back
Look back down the years
Doesn't help, it appears.

Looking On
Spectating's less living,
More simply existing.

Love's Chemistry
Lovers' temerity
Stems from their chemistry.

Lucky Poets
Lucky poets do well
To have wives who can spell.

Lunar Landing
We can't guess who's handling
The next lunar landing.

Mathematicians
Great mathematicians
Are quasi magicians.

Mayor
The status of mayor
Is beyond compare.

Mirrors
Lack of vanity only
Makes mirrors feel lonely.

Nascent
Nascent's a word
That speaks of birth.

National Wealth
The wealth of a nation's
It's people's donations.

Nature
Despite man's nature,
Nature's his saviour.

Nature's Discards
Basic nature selects
Then discards all the rest.

Nature's Fate
Our greatest danger's
Disrupting nature.

Need
Need's a condition
That leads to sedition.

Never Explain
You don't have to explain
If you've made yourself plain.

New News
If it's not renewed,
The news isn't new.

Non-connections
Failed railway connections
Can wreck reputations.

Non-starter
What negates the word 'go!'
Is a positive 'no!'

Odd Aitch
How perverse, the word 'aitch'
Doesn't start with an aitch.

Overbrevity
Some overbrevity
Challenges clarity.

Paint
Paint's a mere veneer that's
Applied to appearance.

Past Truths
It used to be fact
That the earth was flat.

Philosophy
Pure philosophy is
The theory of theories.

Pickpockets
Some pickpockets use
A queue for their ruse.

Pie and Piglets
Like pie in the sky,
Pink piglets might fly!

Pills
Keep taking the pills
That lessen your ills.

Pips
We should really think hard
About things we discard.

Poetry's Imagery
Plenty of poetry
Lives in its imagery.

Population Satisfaction
Satisfaction for most
Is the Government's boast.

Power
Inordinate power
Makes the timorous cower.

Praises
Refusal of praise
With double repays.

Predicting
Most bids at prediction
Carry least conviction.

Principles
Principles that waver
Compromise behaviour.

Print Matters
What large print promises
Small print diminishes.

Problems
Problems don't arise
With those who are wise.

Progressive Successes
Nothing progresses
Without successes.

Proof
The genius of proof
Is obsessional truth.

Pursuits
For one's every pursuit
There's an optimum route.

Pussy Cunning
When a cat stops preening
We know that it's scheming.

Reacting
Instinctive reactions
Can brook no distractions.

Reading and Learning
Reading and learning
Suit the discerning.

Reciprocal Faith
Reciprocal faith
Is confidence based.

Reflecting Forgiving
One facet of living
Reflects our forgiving.

Regrets
It's hard to forget
The things we regret.

Relaxing Muscles
Let your muscles relax
After vigorous acts.

Resolutions
His New Year vows
Mayn't hers espouse.

Responses
Give truth your welcome,
Mistakes your pardon.

Right Card
If you play the right card,
Winning isn't that hard.

Risible
It may seem risible
Laughter's invisible.

Romancing
Soft music when dancing
Can lead to romancing.

Same Sham
Bestseller's a sham,
Like the groom's best man.

Santa Claus
Santa Claus is one bloke
Who you'll never see smoke

School Fool
If you let down your school
They'll all call you a fool.

Science
Science commenced
With proof's defence.

Scorn
The silence of scorn
Just has to be borne.

Secrecy
When secrecy ceases,
Love's ardour decreases.

Secrets
A secret that's shared
Is a promise dared.

Self-sufficiency
Personal sufficiency's
Living efficiently.

Self-taught
A lesson self-taught
By far's the best sort.

Shared Views
When folk share your views,
They're hard to refuse.

Showers for Hours
Using his-and-hers showers
Entertains them for hours.

Skin Care
When temperatures rise,
Apply your disguise.

Snail
You can trust a snail
To leave a wet trail.

Snaps
A photo unposed
Could double one's woes.

Snoring
It's hard ignoring
Those who are snoring.

Species
Prehistory embraces
The nature of species.

Standards
Once you've set out your stall,
See your standards don't fall.

Strong Language
Language prevails
Where violence fails.

Superfluity
Free gift's as insane
As saying wet rain.

Tan
Her even tan
Intrigues a man.

Taxes
Annual taxation
Pays for the nation.

Tea and Water
Tea and then water
Lead to the loo, sir.

Temper
Bad temper arises
From nasty surprises.

That Glint
With that glint in her eye
She would know he'd comply.

Theory
When theory meets doubt
Tests enter the bout.

Thoughts
Like sardines in a shoal,
Thoughts are hard to control.

Tips
There should be good reason
For tips to be given.

Tropical Choices
Those born in the tropics
Will choose their own topics.

Trouble
Trouble's sure to emerge
When opponents converge.

True Friend
A friend isn't bought
When no return's sought.

Truth
What people opine
Becomes truth in time.

Truths
Truths recognized
Beat lies contrived.

Upset and Downcast
If an upset should last,
It could leave you downcast.

Use and Beauty
Accept what's practical,
Admire what's beautiful.

Useful Reading
When we read what we choose,
What we learn we will use.

Valued Friends
When friends find success,
Don't value them less.

Verbal Contraception
A verbal rejection's
The best contraception.

Verse
A verse a day
Keeps stress away.

Vice and Virtue
Vice is malicious,
Virtue ambitious.

Vital Style
Fashions may change,
But style remains.

Voids
Voids are something
Full of nothing.

Voyeurs
It's the length of her skirt
That keeps voyeurs alert.

Wealthy Outcome
Wealth is the outcome
Of healthy income.

Wear and Tear
Many troubles are born
When components get worn.

Weeks
Weekdays and weekends
Are intimate friends.

Wifely Harness
For the time of your life
Pray don't harness your wife.

Wifely Wealth
A wife acquires wealth
Through her husband's stealth.

Wine Effect
Once wine has been poured,
All rules are ignored.

Winning
Winning is sweeter
When risk's the greater.

Words Ignored
Some words we ignore
Are worth using more.

Yawn
As a matter of form,
One tries not to yawn.

Yellow Peril
Bananas you've fed on
Are skins you might slip on.

CHAPTER 37 with 206 two-liners

ODD EXTRACTS

Aerial Snoopers
They drone and moan underneath the cumulus,
Their trespassing pilots snooping around us.

Ample
Ample can vary from just enough
To bearing some superfluous stuff.

Arguments
Our strength has many manifestations,
Not least by way of argumentation.

Attitudes
The pessimist's seized by futile dubiety;
His opposite's free to seize opportunity.

Awareness
Man can only to known things aspire;
Thus awareness delimits desire.

Barking Dog
When a dog is left in the garden to bark,
It always shouts loudest when kept in the dark.

Beard Wise
Bearding a person involves confrontation:
Confronting a beard might cause apprehension.

Best Pleasures
Resources of pleasure are widely deployed:
Often least expected are most enjoyed.

Biennial
A biennial happens both this year and next:
What's biannual, though, into one year's compressed.

Bigotry
Bigotry laughs in the face of reason,
Stuck in its ways with defiant adhesion.

Bin Men
Those chaps you've seen working from bin to bin
In time will profit from what you've dropped in.

Boredom
His practical way to avoid being boring
Was watching for signs of the onset of snoring.

Brevity
From skimpy nighties to short winter days,
Brevity works in innumerable ways.

Bridge of Love
Their arms outstretched to either bank,
They keep a link from flank to flank.

Bridges
Bridges are built for linking two sides;
The finest will vaunt their stature besides.

Carpets
Those fitted carpets we cut to shape
Are vast creators of fibrous waste.

Chance It
Proceeding to build without permission
Is worth the risk, says oral tradition.

Chance Remarks
How often we spot that a chance remark
Succeeds in igniting that vital spark

Choices
A choice is always ours to make,
And hard when there's a lot at stake.

Christmas Gifting
When you're searching for gifts to give at Christmas,
You're sure to find it an endless business.

Christmas Trees
Dressed Christmas trees suffer by being so small:
Having lost their young roots they wither and fall.

Columbus
When Columbus and crew went cruising along,
It appears that they'd got their bearings all wrong.

Comme Ci, Comme Ça
'Twixt glad and sad sits a median ground:
Neither happiness smiles, nor sadness frowns.

Compost
Deriding the compost where insects crawl,
Some deem it waste though it isn't at all.

Conclusions
Sooner than seek correct solutions,
People leap to the wrong conclusions.

Cornice
When a cornice connects the wall to the ceiling,
It gives the whole room an elegant feeling.

Country and Town
Beautiful countryside. City and town:
One fashioned on high. The others low down.

Critical Acclaim
If all of the critics damned us the same,
We'd not know the phrase 'to critical acclaim'.

Critical Eye
Having a critical eye
Needn't mean good things slip by.

Critical Hints
The tiniest hint of satire can serve
To teach the lesson some critics deserve.

Curiosity's Lure
Curiosity's lure can tempt the unwitting
Into situations they find unbefitting.

Danger
It's rarely something falls from the skies;
Home is the place where most danger lies.

Dehumidification
Dehumidification
Can repel condensation.

Delays
Delays and postponements might give us the hump,
Unless they're just giving us time to catch up.

Demagogues
With verve the demagogue's urging inspires
The people to serve his selfish desires.

Democratic Debate
When a nation's people are given a voice,
They just can't stop talking, debating a choice.

Detectorist
Watch the dectorist scanning a beach,
And hope the odd landmine is out of his reach.

Devotion
Devoting oneself to a course of action
Merits a measure of satisfaction.

Diamond Jubilee
That was a day of great jubilation
When all rejoiced with the Queen of the Nation.

Diary
A diary's a mixture of feelings and facts,
With intimate details the things it most lacks.

Dignity and Impudence
Dignity mounts a stallion's hide:
Impudence takes an ass for a ride.

Direction
A slight divergence or deviation
Will doubtless mean a change of direction.

Dirty Splashes
While your patio's cleaned, being powerjet sprayed,
Dirty adjacent splashes are sure to be made.

Disclosures
What gall, and poverty of soul, have those
Who oath-sworn promises blithely disclose.

Discoveries
Discoveries aren't all made by explorers:
Penicillin was found right there before us.

Discretion
Honesty features in all our lives;
In truth it's where discretion applies.

Distances
Views in close propinquity might not delight:
Hills are majestic the more distant the sight.

Dithering
Prevarication debates the question;
Procrastination delays the action.

DIY Problems
Sometimes DIY can become overcoming,
Like when something's gone wrong with the plumbing.

Doers and Booers
Those who create could liken their critics
To crowds in stands who never take wickets.

Do-gooder
To be a do-gooder isn't as fine as
Doing good things when occasion arises.

Doing Good
At times one wonders if they should
Apply their life to doing good.

Done and Dumb
The done thing's an act we happily sanction;
The dumb thing provokes a hapless reaction.

Dreams
A dream is like a DVD
Not known but picked out randomly.

Ducking
'To duck' derives from a bird that's upended
But mayn't protect what's barely defended.

Duration
Women mostly just won't wait a minute;
Only pregnancy lengthens their limit.

Earthly Invasions
Agronomists now, with few inhibitions,
Invade the pure earth with lethal additions.

The Easy Way
If something's confusing, we tend to complain
And leave to those with more nous to explain.

Elasticity
Elasticity stretches then retracts,
Lets you sit up straight or choose to relax.

The Element of Surprise
Leaving earth and wind, fire and water aside,
The fifth and last element's that of surprise.

Enforcing
Pressure's applied as a means of enforcing;
Agreements involve a degree of endorsing.

Enigma
An enigma's nought but a puzzling notion:
A riddle that lives till its code is broken.

Enthusiasms
Enthusiasms, how quickly they change:
We used to be keen to watch aeroplanes.

Equilibrium
When equilibrium loses its balance,
It's up against a restorative challenge.

Exasperation
Frustration engenders exasperation
Whose only solution is inspiration.

Explanations
Explanations are something that help us to learn;
Intimations remain of much lesser concern.

Expressive Impressions
Expressions don't relate to impressions
Except as personal impersonations.

Extension Pretension
We often see houses that boast an extension.
It is isn't a need, it stems from pretension.

Fait Accompli
When each understands the other one's musing,
No fuller discussion warrants pursuing.

The Future
The future's known input is not worth assessing:
Its sole contribution is keeping us guessing.

Gender's Patience
Calling men most patient is out of the question:
Consider the mother's gestation duration!

Ghosts
People seem frightened of meeting a ghost;
But maybe it's ghosts fear meeting *us* most.

Good and Bad
We learn of good deeds with a hint of surprise:
To news of bad actions acceptance applies.

Good Sense
We're pleased to acknowledge the patent good sense
Of those who concur with our own sentiments.

Good Signs
A smile, a wave, a nod, a wink
Mean more to us than we may think.

Granules
Should you scatter the granules of pure coffee beans,
You'll find gathering them up's far worse that it seems.

Greed
Greed is desiring beyond what you need,
Even those things you'd have others concede.

Guess or Assess
Less complicated than calculation,
Estimates favour approximation.

Gullible Sceptic
To pose as both sceptic and as believer
Is like being well when suffering a fever.

Heads for Content
With flicks of coins our fates will decide:
Heads for content, tails for dissatisfied.

Heart and Head
When heart and head concur with each other,
That's the day when decisions break cover.

Hills and Vales
Viewed from the dales, the hills are majestic;
Seen from the peaks, the vales a mosaic.

Honour
True honour is something that money can't buy,
Nor can it recover if things go awry.

Icons
Icons used to receive religious attention:
Now they only acquire a secular mention.

Impartial Assessment
People who place themselves over the rest
Haven't as yet been correctly assessed.

Improvisation
Lacking the ease of pre-preparation,
Interviewees face improvisation.

Instants
An instant can trigger a lengthy event,
Achieving a target not otherwise meant.

Integrity
Integrity's demons, pride and pretence,
Need dedication to aid its defence.

Interaction
As thanks rely on the presence of kindness,
Happiness thrives on the absence of sadness.

Interest
Interest's out of two elements made:
Enthusiasm and profit that's paid.

Intuition
Spontaneous feminine intuition
Complements masculine reasoned conviction.

Ironing
The reason we sprinkle cold water on clothing
Is mainly to see how the ironing's going.

Kitchen Tray
If your kitchen tray has a slippery base,
It's hard to avoid odd crockery escapes.

Lacking Ideas
When think-tanks are needed for finding ideas,
There are not enough mouths but too many ears.

Limits
Once given a task you strive to complete it
Until you reach your ability's limit.

Locale
Signs of where we were born, and later raised,
Appear in one's speech and typical ways.

Lofty Risk
No lofty storage beneath a roof
Should lightly be viewed as vermin-proof.

Loneliness
Despite the thousands residing in towns,
The plight of loneliness sadly abounds.

Loner
Discreetly informed he was out on a limb,
He reformed himself and mixed more with his kin.

Loquacity
Imagine a parrot incessantly squawking,
Then envisage MPs persistently talking.

Losing the Toss
One man's gain is another man's loss;
Some might care, others don't give a toss.

Loved Ones
We hasten to welcome occasional guests
While lacking regard for the ones we love best.

A Matter of Gender
Women are known for their intuition:
Men for their scientific cognition.

Men and Boys
Kite-boards and muscles, jet-skis and toys;
They certainly sort the men from the boys.

Moral Fence
A moral fence bears a difficult plight:
It has to divide what's wrong from what's right.

Mysterious Objects
Mysterious objects high in the sky
Provided film buffs with books they could buy.

Myth and Mystery
Myth and mystery are jointly mistaken:
People pay neither serious attention.

Necessity
When a need arises we improvise,
Necessity driving our enterprise.

Net Wisdom
Information's accessed via the Net,
But wisdom isn't implanted there yet.

New Opinions
Like smoking fish strung out to cure,
New opinions have to mature.

Niggle
An odd itch that becomes a persistent niggle
At times can induce an embarrassing wriggle.

No Option
Whatever the cause of a raging storm,
It's something that simply has to be borne.

Normality
Normality isn't a stable state:
Its nature changes as standards dictate.

Notoriety
One of the options for notoriety
Is breaking into higher society.

The Odd Mistake
Just as old Homer would sometimes nod,
We all occasionally need a prod.

Odium
Comparing one thing with another
Needn't bring odium down on either.

Offensive
Raising a fence that's rather extensive
Tends to put neighbours on the defensive.

Old Habits
Old habits die hard and disappear,
Replaced by others we'll soon hold dear.

Old Memories
The recycling shop that's close to the gate
Sells old memories discarded of late.

Opportunities
Sly opportunities act like opponents,
Timing their strikes at inopportune moments.

Outreach
Outreach pertains to those useful connections
Communities share with organisations.

Over and Under
Overestimation's an error we make,
And underperformance the causal mistake.

Partings
Partings are predicated on meetings,
Trusting to safe reunions' greetings.

Partnership
One asks questions, the other explains;
The pendulum swings, so neither gains.

Patience
Patience is the art of waiting
Till the moment's ripe for taking.

Paying a Visit
A pair of options is quite exquisite:
Saying toodle-oo or paying a visit.

Pebbles
Most pebbles on beaches are beautifully smooth,
Unlike inland boulders that can't even move.

Perfectionism
Perfectionists note the tiniest flaw
The average person's inclined to ignore.

Planets and Stars
Heavenly bodies like Venus and Mars
Are often confused with silver-screen stars.

Pole Star
As long as the pole star knows where its place is,
It's sure to retain the status of stasis.

Possessions
Impressive possessions make men of repute;
Such qualifications, though, many refute.

Postscript
The nub of a letter's effectively placed
In a postscript note, the most prominent space.

Prodigality
The prodigal vagrant, on pleasures intent,
Returned both with wealth and his health overspent.

Projects
A latent project needs activation;
No fuse will ignite by inclination.

Promises
A promise you make is a kind of debt:
Once entered into, it has to be met.

Prospective Comfort
Comfort's a prospect we all have in view,
And when it's elapsed we try to renew.

Questionable
Whatever is questionable leaves you unsure:
It depends on confirming a good deal more.

Questioning
Persistent questions in conversation
Are more akin to interrogation.

Queueing
Queueing not knowing if you'll get in;
That's when patience begins to wear thin.

Quick Wit
A savant, reversing start and conclusion,
Can find a problem for any solution.

Quills
Some time since birds changed the shape of their bills,
Writers took feathers to use as their quills.

Quits
A good example of calling things quits
Is when opponents agree to desist.

Quorum
When members assemble with business before them,
Committees must muster at least a full quorum.

Reciters
What others have writ, or allegedly said,
Great speakers recite off the top of their head.

Recompense
Your recompense for kindness spread
Is sleeping peacefully in bed.

Reflections
Should we catch a reflection and stupidly gawk,
It's relieving to know that our mirrors can't talk.

Relief
As soon as his note emerged from the shredder,
Her surge of conscience got suddenly better.

Respectability
Respectability comes in a package
The merest breach of decorum would damage.

Returns
Echoes and mirrors both bounce things back;
Publishers, too, have acquired the knack.

The Right Moment
When you pick the right moment, you waste least time:
Unoccupied waiting distresses the mind.

Rights of Way
Ramblers go trekking with rucksacks and boots
While farmers challenge their rights-of-way routes.

Risky Changes
Fools alter things for change's sake,
Despite the risks they know they take.

River
We bathe, baptise, and cast the fish's lure,
Yet not an instant may its state endure.

The River of Time
The river of time sweeps debris away;
It's nature's scheme for removing decay.

The Rock
The tortured rock, disfigured by time,
Is now beleaguered by those who climb.

Rolling Things Out
They'll roll out just about anything now,
From sanitized carpet to sacred cow.

Rules and Regulations
If regulations differ from rules,
It may be the same with idiots and fools.

Rural Communities
Our rural communities used to thrive;
Due to invaders, they barely survive.

Saying and Writing
Things you say might sound impolite;
More risky, though, are things you write.

Scarf
Wearing a scarf to protect your chest
Just goes to show that mother knows best.

The Scrounger's Mantra
The mantra for scroungers endorses their plan:
Wherever you are, cadge as much as you can.

Seconds
Seconds eventually turn into minutes,
But keeping count of them does have its limits.

Sharp Corners
Sharp corners must rate as a bane of our lives:
No sooner we've struck them than bruises arise.

Shelf Life
A shelf life has little to do with shelves:
No more than the life part belongs to the elves.

Silence's Weight
Light-hearted banter comes loud and clear;
The weight of silence impresses the ear.

Skylines
City skylines are made of rectangular chunks,
Often with oddly-shaped architectural lumps.

Skyscrapers
As you watch the next skyscraper reaching up high,
You can only gawp upward and ask yourself why.

Sleeping Time
Going to sleep marks the end of the day:
The clock, however, keeps ticking away.

Small Deeds
Among kind acts that mean the most is
Each small deed that passes unnoticed.

Sniffers and Quaffers
Adhesives have had their solvents removed;
Alcohol, though, is discreetly approved.

Social Stress
Affected by changes they cannot arrest,
People today are excessively stressed.

Solar Panels
With solar panels adorning the roof
We're led to believe we're inflation proof.

Stammers
People with stammers quite frequently find
They're given more time to make up their mind.

Standing and Staring
Even when nothing and nobody's there,
Times come when we inwardly stand and stare.

Statistics
Statistics are gathered like grapes from a vine
But their use, unlike wine, is hard to define.

Straight Lines
Nature's not keen on seeing straight lines:
Canals and railways are men's designs.

Strangers
On meeting, strangers are mostly polite:
It's keeping that way that's hard to get right.

Style
Style's either innate or later acquired;
Whichever applies, it's highly desired.

Styles
Most agile people can climb a stile;
Needing a stick, a gate's more your style.

Suggestions
Suggestions are things we'd like to see tried;
Objections try to have notions decried.

Sunlight and Rain
While sunlight promotes the growth of grain,
Exponentially so does the rain.

Surfaces
Tough, as in leather, is all to the good;
But rough reminds us of unsanded wood.

Symbiosis
A mixture of words can invoke a whole scene:
A picture spurs words to interpret its theme.

Talent
Whatever training and practice entailed,
His natural talent always prevailed.

Tastes and Urges
Our tastes and urges, so widely ranging,
Throughout the years remain ever changing.

Tectonics
After our planet's primordial birth,
Tectonic plates have shaped most of the earth.

Text Test
When documents use such diminutive text,
An eyeglass is something we'd like to possess.

Tit for Tat
The landsman dismisses the pleasures of sailing;
The sailor finds landscapes too little availing.

Tools
Most of the animals take us for fools:
They leave it to man to make all the tools.

Toothpaste
Those squeezed-out stripes on a dentifrice brush
Over the decades have cost us too much.

Traditions
Modern traditions are mostly commercial,
And most of the old ones quite controversial.

Treasure Album
The mind is an album with pictures replete,
Each image a treasure one couldn't repeat.

Umpteenth
Umpteenth means that, without any doubting,
Somebody simply hasn't been counting.

Unexpected Reactions
Unexpected reactions sometimes lead
To querying things we erstwhile believed.

Unexpected Silence
His unuttered oration
Didn't match the ovation.

Unhappiness
Unhappiness lies in a latent state
That's activated by triggers of fate.

Validation
On validated statements we'll always rely:
Unwarranted assumptions can too often lie.

Visualization
By using our minds we can visualize
Things we can't figure when using our eyes.

Vowing
Watching a guardsman who's standing erect
Reminds us of vows we mustn't neglect.

War and Love
To claim all's fair in war and love
Is not a message couched above.

Wasting Time
Many odd items that live in a cupboard
Stay wasting their time till they're rediscovered.

Ways and Means
The meaning of tantrum is wanting it now;
The meaning of scheming is working out how.

Weakness and Strength
Weakness relies on guile and a prank,
While strength alone is open and frank.

Who do you think you are?
The question of who do think you are
Can only be answered by probing afar.

Wood and Timber
Wood's a rough material gleaned from trees:
Timber's an outcome that meets people's needs.

Your Presence
Wherever you are, you must agree
Present is where you happen to be.

CHAPTER 38 with 35 two-liners

ON REFLECTION

Canvas
When the breadth of your canvas just isn't enough,
You might have to resort to some two-sided stuff.

Debater
Because he's considered a decent debater,
He has to stand up be it sooner or later.

Distant Skies
Though they say we can't see beyond the horizon,
There are distant skies we can focus our eyes on.

Earth's Worth
You can purchase a plot of mother earth
Without really knowing what it is worth.

Four Somes
Some people know some things while some know others,
And some know it all one swiftly discovers.

Hindrances
Hindrances constantly get in the way,
Whether on purpose one can't always say.

Improper Advice
To say that lightning won't strike a place twice,
Sounds like imparting improper advice.

In Sync
A pendulum swings in sync with time:
Time is the governor, not the chime.

In Trouble
Getting in trouble, albeit concerning,
Certainly's one of the best ways of learning.

Incognito
What a strain, all those years in achieving acclaim;
Now it's please, may she go incognito again.

Inferiority
Feeling inferior dents one's prestige;
So countermand it, and get off your knees.

Inklings
Sometimes it's wise to release just an inkling,
And keep inside the full gist of your thinking.

Insult and Injury
An injury lasts its allotted extent:
An insult's a longer-enduring event.

Knowledge and Wisdom
While Foraging Knowledge is briefed to roam,
The Wizard of Wisdom stays chiefly at home.

Learn First
Look before leaping and think before speaking
Are tenets we learn and stay in our keeping.

Mistakes
Though you might prefer to hide your mistakes,
They've made you wiser and that's no disgrace.

Mistakes and Flaws
A self-evident fact we tend to ignore
Is our every mistake exposes a flaw.

Mind Weeding
If I could weed my memory's bed,
I'd first reject the rubbish I've read.

Mockery
Derision of others might not be wise:
Reciprocal mocking often applies.

Mucus
When people need to start blowing their nose,
How can they know where their old mucus goes?

New Formulation
'New formulation' is meant to impress.
But do we get more? More probably less!

Odds Even
A storm cloud needn't end in rain:
You've still a chance, whatever your game.

The Reader
Please, let me read your poems myself;
I keep a dictionary on the shelf.

Retraction
Should someone induce you to change your mind,
You can always retract if you're so inclined.

Self-knowledge
Those of known importance appear in *Who's Who*;
More important to *you* is you knowing you.

Strength in Numbers
If underperformance weakens a movement,
There may be a case for further recruitment.

Sunlight
We oughtn't to say 'The sun's coming out.'
Really it's clouds that we're talking about.

Traditional Ways
Social experiments tend to fail tests;
Traditional ways are mainly found best.

Transgression
The slightest transgression
Can teach one a lesson.

Troublesome Women
Women are trouble who scheme to manoeuvre
Things they've offered you back in their favour.

Truth to Tell
Facing that phrase: 'To tell the truth', we reflect
On whether what follows we ought to suspect.

Unwitting
Among our deeds that are deemed fulfilling
There must be some we achieve unwitting.

Volunteers
Volunteering relieves what's terribly boring,
Or else it reveals people's courage when warring.

Wearisome Tedium
Some tedious days follow wearisome nights,
Until with relief they refocus their sights.

Wisdom
While wisdom insists on sound information,
Good judgement's a stronger qualification.

CHAPTER 39 with 85 two-liners

POETRY

Absorbing Verse
Thinking absorbs the inquisitive mind:
Absorbing poems leave worries behind.

Acuity
Poems revealing astute acuity
Seem destined to last in perpetuity.

Anthologies
Anthologists muster the same old verses,
Depriving their readers of wider resources.

Anti-verse
Her verse contrived a succession of lines
Comprising no meaning, metre or rhymes.

Cadence and Rhyme
Though cadence and rhyme can loosen their tether,
It's patently clear they're better together.

Cerebrum
If you write two lines and give them a title,
At least you will know your brain isn't idle.

Christmas Rhythm
Poems on Christmas cards often lack rhythm;
Given a year, that can't be forgiven.

Concealing Knowledge
Some poets are people who know a great deal,
But treat it as something they ought to conceal.

Deprivation
A poke at a poet's cold deprivation
Can stoke the coals of his inspiration.

Don't Tell All
Don't tell them it all, ensure there's some doubt
As to what your poem is all about.

Emerging Verse
A poem emerges through changes of mind,
Until its true meaning is clearly defined.

Epigram
An epigram should be petite,
And, hopefully, with wit replete.

Epigrammatic Conclusions
Often we find that a classical sonnet
Concludes with an epigram hanging from it.

Epigrams
In very few words the epigram lifts
The lid on innumerable human gifts.

Feigned Astuteness
Some verse perversely dupes by obtuseness,
Lack of clarity feigning astuteness.

Flower Power
After honing his verses for hours and hours,
She'll sometimes prefer him to say it with flowers.

Free-Versers
It's said the free-verser complains too much,
Unlike the rhymester contented as such.

Gleaning Meaning
Though poems' titles give some indication,
The reader seeks further interpretation.

Grief Relief
Some poetry focuses only on grief.
One only hopes poets find love a relief.

Her Stanzas
Her every line was precisely sculpted;
Hence immaculate stanzas resulted.

Iambics
Iambic beginnings to any poems
At least let you know the way they'll be going.

Memorable Rhyme
The lines we remember time after time
Are the ones invested in memorable rhymes.

Mimesis
Creative language acclaimed as poetic
Tends to be echoed in writings mimetic.

Obit
Her later works, like polished pebbles honed,
For early rough and jagged verse atoned.

Odd Odes
Poetic oddities stem from teachers
Less happy to write than act as preachers.

Pause for Thought
When poets like Keats had thoughts to convey,
They always, poetically, found a way.

Personal Verse
Mass production and mass consumption
Aren't the nature of poetry's function.

Philosophers
Philosophers tend to be poets as well,
Esoteric pretence thereby to dispel.

Philosophical Poetry
Heavy sessions of thought should be interspersed
With relaxing confections of lighter verse.

Poems and Sewing
Whether she takes to his latest poem
Depends on how well her sewing's been going.

Poesy
In nature's great creative scheme
Only poesy lets you dream.

Poet
A poet has to be twice a man:
A writer, also a music man.

Poet Laureate
It's the testing task of the present laureate
To find another acceptable poet.

Poetic Apostrophes
At times when we meet a verbal catastrophe
We try to locate a subtle apostrophe.

Poetic Apprentice
To both the mature and untutored apprentice,
Creating a verse can be labour-intensive.

Poetic Contention
Throughout her days she voiced the contention
That versing was pleasure, not a profession.

Poetic Contentment
Poetry deals with the essence of things;
Hence, the essential contentment it brings.

Poetic Emotions
In releasing instinctive feelings we cloak,
Poems' words are those our emotions evoke.

Poetic Expression
Emotions seeking articulation
Feel the need of poetic expression.

Poetic Frustration
Readers of poems find it frustrating
When most of the wording needs explaining.

Poetic Gestation
In the effort approaching a poem's birth
Rhyme is the midwife assisting the verse.

Poetic Imagery
A poem with imagery livens the reader
By giving content an active demeanour.

Poetic Insights
Poems are places where life is displayed:
Compacted insights the poets have made.

Poetic Legacy
Each poem's the gift of somebody's mind,
An intimate legacy left behind.

Poetic Mistake
She hung a rhyme on the end of a line,
Attempting her prose as verse to define.

Poetic Oasis
Distant from bleak platitudinous places,
Versing appears like a fertile oasis.

Poetic Successes
When syntax expressively text compresses,
One's poems perchance may meet with successes.

Poetic Trade
Verse trades in rhythm and metaphor's guile,
In irony's wit and simile's style.

Poetic Translation
The words that we choose in poetic translation
Risk changing the gist of the poet's conception.

Poetical Metre
The regular cadence of words he'll choose
Is due to the iambs he's prone to use.

Poetry
The way we like to speak and what we try to say
When we've time to think and choose words as we may.

Poetry and Prose
Minds that thrive on deciphering poetry
Find reading novels a pleasing novelty.

Poetry with Rhyme
Some say that poetry doesn't need rhyme,
But most agree be it yours or mine.

A Poet's Mantra
Carry a pen and a pad of paper,
Then words can't vanish in puffs of vapour.

Political Correctness
Now that correctness has studied its part,
Verse is becoming a genderless art.

Pretentiousness
Pretentious people express a shine for
Cryptic poems they'll never decipher.

Prime Rhyme
All poets must notice, when reaching their prime,
That skirt and alert make a natural rhyme.

Purple Lines
Poets seek lines of a purple hue;
I'm nearly there with one red, one blue.

Readings
When a poem's read out by the poet,
Just speak up if you already know it.

Reciting Verse
A certain unease occurs
When poets recite their verse.

Rescuing Rhyme
When poets can't find an accurate rhyme,
Assonance rescues them many a time.

Retro Verse
His poetry plays a retro air
Called 'tis and 'twas and always say ne'er.

Rhyming
This writing in rhyme is all very fine,
Except for the time to refine each line.

Rhythm and Rhyme
An epigram lacking rhythm and rhyme
Is hard to recall, however sublime.

Rich Syllables
A poet once said that after the sun
Between the sheets rich syllables were won.

Schemers
Written by schemers who deem themselves poets
Are pieces by people who yearn to be noticed.

Senselessness
Some poetry speaks but has nothing to say;
Though the words sound right, they've no sense to convey.

Shaggy Dog
A shaggy-dog poem is hard to endure;
An epigram's slick, like a Labrador.

Shakespeare's Sonnets
One fifty-four sonnets. How can you choose
When every one of them lights the same fuse?

Shreds of Poetry
A million poems have passed through my shredder;
If only I'd known how to patch them together!

Size Matters
Epic verses hours assuage:
Bite-size poems match our age.

Slamming
If you're hearing poetry read with elan,
It's a competition that's known as a slam.

Sonic Lines
Savour the rhythm as much as the words,
For what's been written is musical verse.

Stanza
To a question raised on a badly shaped stanza,
A new foot could provide a metrical answer.

Sublime Rhyme
One way of showing that poems need rhyme
Is ending this verse with something sublime.

Syntax Tactics
Occasionally poets resemble an auger,
Twisting their syntax into odd order.

Timely Epigrams
Limiting their notions to minimal lines,
Epigrams are poems befitting our times.

Up for Grabs
Words of advice poets toss in the air
Are up for grabs by whoever may care.

Veiled Verse
No poems conjure so much pride
As those which in one's head reside.

Versification
After working some verse then mulling it over,
He was frequently seen asleep on his sofa.

Versing Aloud
Verse should be served in a version of speaking
Assisting listeners to glean what they're seeking.

Writing in Rhyme
This writing in rhyme is all very fine
Except for the time to refine each line.

Writing Time
I savour my time forsaking sleep,
Creating verse for others to keep.

Yesteryear's Poets
When yesteryear's poets composed their sonnets,
They couldn't depend on copyright profits.

Young Minds
Children sense metre in nursery rhymes
And relish the theatre in pantomimes.

CHAPTER 40 with 78 two-liners

QUERIES

Absolutely
Why should 'absolutely' be used instead
Of that simple word, the adequate 'yes'?

Ale
How many mad drunkards have caused an affray?
And how many more warnings must we convey?

Antonyms
Each concept requires a reciprocal mate:
If love didn't exist, how could we know hate?

Ash Tree
Why does an ash tree remind one of fire?
The poet would say, 'It rhymes with desire.'

Atrophy
When the early bird writes his biography,
Does he assume the rest is just atrophy?

Beer Bits
If beer is a mixture of barley and hops,
Why can't they be openly purchased in shops?

Bees
How did bees manage before they had hives?
Seeing them come must have been a surprise.

Canine Concern
Your pooch just caught its ball in flight:
Was that a task or sheer delight?

Canine Signs
May bitches pass where dogs are banned?
It's hard to know, the way things stand.

Cats
If you find a nice cat that's all alone
Would you shoo it off or give it a home?

Celebrities
Why should celebrities engender a fuss?
They're just doing a job like the rest of us.

Complaints
When the folly around us is past constraint,
To whom, we might ask, do we send our complaint?

Digital Fodder
Where are politeness, courtesy, honour?
Gone to the realm of digital fodder.

Dodos and Dinosaurs
If history repeats itself, like people say,
Will dodos and dinosaurs come back one day?

Dubiety
Though it's perfectly clear a crook's been cheating,
Who knows when a pear is ready for eating?

Eden
She had a cleavage, and *he* had a spout;
But which succeeded in working things out?

English Rose
England's rose was chosen for colours and scents,
So why pick a flower with spiky defence?

Enough Fluff
Why should such words as rough, tough and enough
Have endings that sound like that in pure fluff?

Expert Advice
For expert advice we're obliged to pay.
From friends it's gratis, but is it OK?

Fanning
When latter-day ladies fluttered their fan,
Was it for cooling or coaxing a man?

Favoured Fur
Of all the trials that unfairly occur,
Why doesn't dandruff affect a cat's fur?

First Person
First among equals he's said to be;
So are they all as warlike as he?

Gentlewomen
Some years gone by, gentlewomen were banned.
Was that conceivably gentlemen-planned?

Go
Tell me, why does 'go' pretend to be 'gow'?
It isn't the same with 'to' as we know.

Grandma's Enigma
Grandma sits with a book in her lap;
Is she reading, or taking a nap?

Greenhouse Gasses
Is all this tattle of greenhouse gasses
Just a hustle to rattle the masses?

Hairdos
Why do some menfolk crop off their hair
When evolution planted it there?

Hares
Why do hares box in the first days of spring?
Their urges mimic mad bouts in the ring.

Hole Without End
A bottomless pit serves nobody's role;
Just who would covet an infinite hole?

Insemination
Can Mother Earth, in daily rotation,
Sustain the growth of insemination?

Jumping Lambs
Spring lambs may appear to be jumping for joy,
Or is it their way to beg food they employ?

Know-how
Inadequate skill can trigger a crisis;
How do you know when your know-how suffices?

Laughter
How is a laugh induced by a comic?
It must be a process anatomic.

Let You Read
What good a wife who won't concede
An hour of life to let you read?

Live in Today
Isn't it best to live in today
In case tomorrow won't come our way?

Loving Life
Can they who have reached the end of their span
Without love, have lived as well as man can?

Monkey Business
If man from monkey once derived,
Why are there monkeys still alive?

Moonshine
Did men invade then one small step descend?
That question remains for the moonshine to end.

Naming Game
History repeats itself teacher once said;
So why's grandpa Rupert, and my name's Fred?

Nightingale
Why should the nightingale win such acclaim
While other birds attract much meaner fame?

No Joking
Now wives and girlfriends gather as 'wags',
What will denote the crackers of gags?

Novel Idea
How can a novel be dubbed a bestseller
Before all its pages are put together?

Noxious Merchandise
What worth do they set on human lives
Who fail to mark noxious merchandise?

On Meeting
After 'Hi!' why is it the weather's most frequent?
Because it's the topic with least disagreement!

On the Fence
When next door's windfalls drop in my garden,
Should I say 'thanks' or should *they* beg pardon?

Opinion
Opinion is gauged by the powers that be;
But who do they question? They've never asked me!

Order, Order!
Whenever the Speaker calls for order,
Is it his voice or just a recorder?

The Page Age
Whatever became of the paperless era?
Though it made a great start, it's come nowhere nearer.

Painting Views
How can a painting give life to a view?
Methinks from the artist that answer is due.

Pause to Read
What price your life if, fraught with greed,
You find no time to pause and read?

Picking and Choosing
If you were selecting a pair of shoes,
Would you say pick or would you say choose?

Plan to Read
What use a man whose jobs impede
Your every plan to sit and read?

Poetic Licence
Should gardeners ever make judgements on poems?
Only those knowing their prosodic onions.

Points of View
So, a fan's a gadget for cooling the head?
No, fans are fanatics who never see red!

Poodle Face
If a poodle looks at you rarely blinking,
How can you possibly tell what it's thinking?

Presenters
Why do presenters, who simply communicate,
Seem to know more than those who participate?

Privilege
How does one rate the privileged few?
It's those with more clout than me or you.

Sand
What's the attraction of sand on a beach?
It tells you that work is well out of reach.

Sea Bass
Why had those who named sea bass to interfere?
To separate water from something like beer.

Seasons
Why did every three months become a season?
Nobody seems to remember the reason.

Sizing Up
When trees can reach a hundred feet tall,
What makes a buttercup grow so small?

Sneeze
Among the questions the puzzle books keep
Is 'How can we sneeze when we're fast asleep?'

Strands
What is it makes people recolour their hair?
It ranges from folly through fame to despair.

Tax Men
What is the practice that tax men hate most?
They're handed their bills to save on the post.

Tax People
Now here's an odd query you'll not often hear:
Do tax people curse when their tax bills appear?

Teaser
Fur coat, no knickers? It may be so;
But how, I pray, are you meant to know?

Tell Me
Tell me why on earth with peace my creed
I've to shoot my cuffs and kill my speed?

Time to Read
What price your life if, fraught with greed,
You find no time to pause and read?

Tipping
Why should drivers of taxis expect a tip?
After all it's the owner who financed each trip.

Unbelief
Do atheists consider the need to ensure
There's no other belief they'd wish to abjure?

Unlikelihood
Who knows how riches turn into wealth?
The answer's unlikely to be oneself.

Variable Interest
Variable interest on a fixed rate bond?
One can only wonder where they went wrong.

Variety's Mystery
What makes a daffodil grow so small
When oaks can reach a hundred feet tall?

Vulnerable Gulls
Where seagulls gather and clamour for bread,
Are low birds spattered by those overhead?

Weather People
Weather girls, but weather men;
Why not weather women, then?

Whither the Weather?
Miscellaneous weather's a blithering pest:
Should you go back to sleep, or shower and get dressed?

Wordmonger
The sort of question he'd ask, as a hoot,
Was 'When does a soothsayer say his sooth?'

Words
What use are words if they don't convey
Precisely what we want them to say?

CHAPTER 41 with 14 two-liners

RELIGION

Ancient Myths
The ancient myths were incredible fictions
That served as proxy to modern religions.

Conciliation
Every religion has written its chapter;
Together the essence of peace they capture.

Conviction
Prior to Darwin, most clung to religion;
Some have since switched to another conviction.

Custom
Through accustomed routines, by his own admission,
He used superstition in lieu of religion.

Existentialism
Existentialism renounces God's licence,
Replacing religion with strict self-reliance.

Faith
Worries assail me, health sometimes fails me,
Conscience unveils me, faith will avail me.

Fractious Days
Something's perverse these fractious days:
Religion kills more than it saves.

Harmonization
Divergent beliefs without toleration
Beg urgent attempts at harmonization.

One Deity
In space and time one deity reigns.
Though races stake their special claims.

Preaching
Had the preacher assumed a humbler mien,
More moved might his congregation have been.

Proselytization
Inducing a person to change their mind
May not in the end turn out to be kind.

Religion and Fiction
Sceptics and atheists challenge religion;
Their gods and devils are treated as fiction.

Thanks
When people declare it's a wonderful day,
They might take a moment to kneel down and pray.

Unbeliever
The unbeliever's unable to find
What theists rely on for peace of mind.

CHAPTER 42 with 27 two-liners

SCIENCE

Apollo's Worth
Among other features displaying its worth,
Apollo 8 showed us the frailty of Earth.

Astral Lands
While comets roam through astral lands,
Alone the pole star static stands.

Cosmos
Man's cosmic knowledge resembles a maze:
It's full of dead ends and endless false trails.

Digital Time
When digital time imposes its powers,
Nine in the evening means twenty-one hours.

Earth's Orbits
When planet Earth's orbits have spasms of lurching,
You'll find more astronomers doing researching.

Experiments
Experiments rarely achieve success,
But each attempt means another one less.

Gnomon Moment
The sundial owns a projecting gnomon
Whose shadow's a self-defining moment.

Heresies
Using evolution of species as proof,
New science makes heresies out of old truth.

Hypotheses
Those mighty hypotheses scientists make
Can suffer the slight of a tiny mistake.

Isosceles Triangles
Isosceles triangles come to a point,
While their opposite corners make the same joint.

Jet Propulsion
What science delivers through jet propulsion
Is criminal loads of lethal pollution.

Lead and Feather
A morcel of lead and a like-weighing feather
Released side-by-side would make landfall together.

Maths
Some discount maths as soulless and boring;
Then the need for it comes without warning.

Nano Era
This is the era of nano technology
When small is in thrall to new opportunity.

Nature's Way
Science tells lies to get its own way;
When nature rejects them, it's we who pay.

Orion's Nebula
Explore the night sky then focus your eye on
The nebula round the sword of Orion.

Progress
Joe Scientist proves another brain wrong;
He'll meet the same fate as time moves along.

Rigidity
While steel and concrete come with rigidity,
Water finds it in constant frigidity.

Science and Art
If science pursues its invasion of art,
We'll surely disparage its lacking of heart.

Scientists
Scientists set religion aside,
Ignoring faults they clearly can't hide.

Scientists and Mystics
Before scientific investigation
Mystics sought truths through intense contemplation.

Shadows
Every shadow depends on light.
You can't disprove it, try as you might.

That String Thing
The only surprise that science could spring
Is finding the length of a piece of string.

Uncertainty
When pundits confer, they concur that, certainly,
Science's weakness is frequent uncertainty.

Vacuum Cleaner
Devoid of all matter, a vacuum's arena
Above any other will turn out the cleaner.

Washing Lines
When clothes on the line play their wrap-around antics,
They're simply obeying the laws of mechanics.

Weeds
Once science discovers its worth to man,
A weed survives through the herbicide ban.

CHAPTER 43 with 18 two-liners

SEASONS

April's Delight
We can all rejoice when April appears,
The month with a voice delighting our ears.

Bitter Sweet
Those bitter winter days are soon replaced
By spring's ever abiding sweeter taste.

Calendar Rotation
Rotating the names of months of the year
Would sometimes make wintertime less severe.

Cares
Once glistening spring has shed winter's hide,
You feel you can cast all your cares aside.

Drab Winter
How drab for us will winter be
When withered leaves have left the trees.

Fall
Our cousins call the autumn 'fall'
Since shedding leaves they can't forestall.

First of May
When April turns its face towards May,
It sees the best, I'm happy to say.

First Rakings
Spring's first rakings expect to confirm
The lawn's alive with emerging worms.

Fresh Thoughts
As winter winds down, to fresh thoughts we cling
Of lengthening days and the joys of spring.

May
Afternoon on a blue summer day
Is at its best when the month is May.

Spring Songs
Daffodils' trumpets awaken the spring,
Inspiring the thrush and blackbird to sing.

Spring's Awakening
Now skylarks are singing on the wing,
We know that it's the awakening of spring.

Spring's Heralds
When singing skylarks above us fly,
Daffodils point their heads to the sky.

Summer Sun
Young fools discover when peeling's begun
The trouble with summer must be the sun.

Verdant May
Each blossoming year when maytime comes round,
The verdant landscape is bursting with sound.

Winter Confusion
Sometimes November can think it's December
With January a second contender.

Wintry Nightfalls
When wintry nightfalls are still drawing in,
They'll frostily wait for spring to begin.

Wonderful May
Eagerly waiting for wonderful May,
Let April wash March's litter away.

CHAPTER 44 with 58 two-liners

SPORT

Adrenalin
Once their adrenalin starts to kick in,
Footballers fancy they're going to win.

Advance Bookings
When football fixtures start to be played,
Christmas arrangements have to be made.

All-round Sportsman
Whoever it was invented the ball
Was surely the greatest sportsman of all.

Amateurs
The fact that most amateurs don't get paid
Needn't detract from the way the game's played.

Anglers
Obsessively hooked on disputing size,
Addicts who fish tell innocuous lies.

Bad Traditions
Old customs don't justify killing for sport.
No statute on earth should such murder support!

Batsmen
Some cricketers fear when they're holding a bat,
Like fish in a bowl being watched by a cat.

Boxer
What a boxer measures from head to his toes
Must have an effect on the length of his blows.

Caber and Shot
From tossing the caber or putting the shot,
Some parts of one's body might throb quite a lot.

Climbers
Heights are for those who relish high climbs,
Keeping vertigo out of their minds.

Coaches
Alas, those best suited to coach national teams
Are sitting with bitters or screaming at screens.

Commentaries
Commentators on matches packed with action
Are sadly a source of constant distraction.

Cricket in Whites
Husbands in white often slip on the green
While wives, out of sight, give trousers a clean.

Cricket's Ashes
Cricket's well known for it's slogs and dashes,
All in the cause of winning the Ashes.

Cricketers' Dreams
When cricketers dream someone's gone off their rocker,
They probably mean he's devoted to soccer.

Croquet and Hockey
Wooden balls on a lawn with hoops for croquet
Watch balls and hooked sticks for playing their hockey.

Cued Up
With no known disputes and no cheats to restrain,
Snooker can claim it's a gentleman's game.

Determination
As athletes know well, determination
Can heighten spectators' expectations.

Devotion to Football
It isn't beyond the bounds of prediction
That football matches could challenge religion.

Divers and Climbers
The ways of divers are quite as precarious
As mountain climbers in various areas.

Fair Bet
Horses don't know that folk bet on who's best,
Else they'd always finish in line abreast.

Football Armour
American football favours full armour;
Regular soccer disdains such palaver!

Formula One
A battle with stresses, a race to be won;
A magical package called Formula One.

Fraught Sport
There's nothing less pure, or more grossly fraught,
Than shooting wild creatures purely for sport.

Gold Medal
To win a gold Olympian medal
Is proof you've shown the strength of your mettle.

Golfing
Striking balls is but part of the passion:
Striking deals is a further attraction.

Hallowed Turf
Kiss Wimbledon's turf if you feel that way;
One wouldn't expect the same thing on clay.

Hunting
Saying that hunting gives humankind pleasure
Tells us some fellows have no heart whatever.

Match Drawn
Cricket in Manchester's subject to rain
That comes to it's rescue now and again.

Monster Golfer
The golfer's a monster on constant patrols
Who hits little balls into innocent holes.

Olympian Ecstasy
The extent of her win was over emphatic;
Overflowing with joy, her state was ecstatic.

Perfect Pitch
A phrase of two words, each starting the same,
Is shared by a diva and cricket game.

Pheasants
Pheasants are raised so that people can shoot them,
Exacting their hideous execution.

Physical Endeavour
To reach the peak of physical endeavour,
Both brain and muscle must function together.

Players
Out on the pitch their names are displayed;
On set or stage they're anonymous made.

Reluctant Golfer
He'd complain that golf made him wander too far
From his favourite place, at the clubhouse bar.

Risks
Danger for some is a challenge they set;
The risks for others they tend to forget.

Risky Snooker
For a woman hovering over a ball
There's a higher risk of a fault being called.

Rugby
There's more to rugby than try-lines alone:
Those oval-shaped balls have minds of their own.

Rugged Rugger
Dismiss the skill and consider reality:
Professional rugby's ruthless brutality.

Rugger Clues
I'd say overall he's one of guys
With an oval ball and muscular thighs.

Second Position
He or she who only came second
Ain't as great as previously reckoned.

Slavery
Though his patient missus saw nothing in it,
Her man, in his whites, was a slave to cricket.

Snooker Shots
They prowl round the table chalking their cues,
Looking for shots they'd be fools to refuse.

Snookered
His cue's no excuse for missing a pot,
And mouthing abuse won't help him a lot!

Soccer
They say that soccer's a beautiful game,
And so it seems if you love to complain.

Soccer on TV
All football matches appear the same,
With bouts of fouling throughout the game.

Soccer Reserve
While you wait on the bench among the reserves,
You might need a bevvy to steady your nerves.

Soccer Stars
With no allegiance to where they enlist,
They play home games where the stadium is.

Sporting Divide
The gentleman's game is played by county:
Ruffians play for a town or city.

Sport's Honour
The ref or umpire was always correct:
Now many a sport's of honour bereft.

Sports
While sports get involved in competition,
They match their skills to some opposition.

Taking Sides
Reminding us of the North-South divide,
Our sports persuade us we have to take sides.

Tennis
Tennis damsels and men compete,
The girls to flirt in skirts petite.

Tennis Elite
The elite who play tennis and win by the set,
Have a roof that enables them not to get wet.

Tennis Menace
The style of his strokes wins great acclaim:
A combination of strength and aim.

Tennis Promise
With a new rubber wall a half inch tall
The old wayward calls would soon be forestalled.

Training
For any young athlete displaying potential,
Bouts of failing to train would prove detrimental.

CHAPTER 45 with 28 two-liners

THEATRE

Actors
Rep actors who play improbable parts
Aren't likely to win their audiences' hearts.

Appearances
Appearances rightly apply to actors;
Reality's fashioned by different factors.

Applause
Much energy's wasted attracting applause
That fickle Joe Public so swiftly ignores.

Articulation
Half the actors portrayed to the nation
Have lost the art of articulation.

Books and Plays
You read a book like driving through traffic:
A play on stage conveys you like magic.

Casting
He'd hold auditions drawing analogies,
Favouring those with stars' similarities.

Clown
With his tragic sadness and furrowed frown,
The world still borrows a laugh from the clown.

Clown Gown
It's probably only a pantomime clown
Who consistently wears an undresssing gown.

Comedy
What thespians proclaim without misgiving,
Is that comedy's the leavening of living.

Comic Deceiver
Comedy plays the part of deceiver,
Making us laugh at our own behaviour.

Concerts
During the interval, patrons stand quaffing:
In between movements they tend to sit coughing.

Dameless
Erasing the dame from a pantomime
Is almost the same as sun without shine.

Dialogue
It's either a prattle of conversation,
Or else a battle of argumentation.

Duels
Dire duels for love, once fought in reality,
Are now meekly sought in theatrical tragedy.

Fallen Star
Once a hot property, glowing with fame,
He suffered the chill of a jealous old flame.

Farce
The boisterous buffoonery labelled as farce
Lies right at the heart of theatrical art.

Improbable Content
According to what the best actors all say,
Improbable content can ruin a play.

Interludes
Interludes offer players a rest,
A time to contemplate what comes next.

Interpretations
Extra thespian fascinations
Stem from actors' interpretations.

Jesting
Since the days of the lute, the jester still thrives
On the happy pursuit of brightening our lives.

Niche
Politicians and actors share a niche
Indulging in histrionics and speech.

Opera
An opera's meaning may lie in its words;
Its message more frequently comes from its verve.

Role Reversal
Compared to transvestite role reversal,
Pantomime dames are non-controversial.

Shakespeare's Words
When Shakespeare proclaimed 'The world is a stage',
His words reflected the thoughts of that age.

Taken In
A meretricious actor might be
Attractive to gullibilty.

Thespian Failing
The actor's state of inebriation
Sadly undid his enunciation.

Thespian Relief
Before the play's first dress rehearsal,
Read some verse for stress reversal!

Vital Statistics
Choices of ladies are made at auditions,
Vital statistics affecting decisions.

CHAPTER 46 with 127 two-liners

TIPS & WRINKLES

Admiration
Admire a person, but don't let them know;
Allow your respect and approval to grow.

Advice
Advice that commences 'If I were you'
Is the kind most people tend to eschew.

Affectation
Affectation won't make you effective:
Its only hope is looking impressive.

Airs and Wrinkles
Refrain from plying your airs and graces:
We all end up with our wrinkled faces.

Altercations
Should altercations last more than a day,
Your peace of mind finds it best to give way.

Alternatives
Options are bound to put pressures on you;
Often it's best to be told what to do.

Ambiguity
Whatever's ambiguous treat with care;
Better be certain than caught unaware.

Anticipation
Beware the anticipation of joy!
Unbidden trouble can pleasure alloy.

Apologies
Apologies often don't say quite enough;
Ensure that your next doesn't rate a rebuff.

Arbitration
When arbitration's the game being played,
Check your trump argument's cogently made.

Argumentation
When two who argue can't banish their plight,
Say both can be wrong and both can be right.

Aspirations
High aspirations that never get met
Are better discarded, without regret.

Assertions
Yes, check if the other's assertion is right,
But note! One dog's bark is another dog's bite.

Avoid the Absurd
With an ill-chosen word or a winner misheard,
It behoves us to try and avoid the absurd.

Be Sure
Be sure, my friend, do not pretend!
Beyond each bend the road might end.

Bias
Prejudice rightly convicts the committer:
Better let evidence act as arbiter.

Biding Time
Impatience risks acting far too soon;
Biding your time could grant you a boon.

Blind Dates
Blind dates can be a dangerous sport;
The risk resides in what might be caught.

Borrowing
A bequest you're allowed in advance to borrow
Remember you may have to forfeit tomorrow.

Claiming Fame
Never claim fame for a race you've won
In case your shoelaces come undone.

Confidences
Rather than risk a confidence broken,
It's better we keep some thoughts unspoken.

Conversation Invasion
On virtually any polite occasion
It's okay to invade a conversation.

Creating Impressions
Always wearing a pleasant expression
Tends to create a fetching impression.

Dancing
Octogenarians, keep on dancing!
An annual ball is life-enhancing.

Delegation
Delegation's a risk one frequently takes;
It's better avoided, to lessen mistakes.

Diet
It's widely believed that we are what we eat,
So when choosing our food we must be discreet.

Disapprobation
Before displaying your disapprobation,
Convince yourself of its justification.

Disputation
In a dispute if you're told to stuff it,
You're wisely advised to rise above it.

Dissembling
The thing we are thinking and what we explain
May differ, dissembling what's really our aim.

Don't Bother
If something goes wrong, one way to act is
Calmly to say don't bother about it.

Drilling
When you're using a drill for making a hole,
Protectors ensure that you'll stay in control.

Dumb Friends
In need of a friend who won't answer back,
Choose an old dog or a new paperback.

Eager Deeds
Eagerness leads to irrational deeds;
It's better to pause and ponder your needs.

Enjoyable Things
There are things you enjoy and those that annoy.
Make sure, if you can, it's the first you deploy.

Euphemism
Should absolute truth risk hurt or offence,
A euphemism could serve as pretence.

Evils
Given two evils from which to choose,
Ask your conscience, then both you'll refuse.

Existing Fruits
While working for things you've still to possess,
Enjoy your existing fruits of success.

Experience
The cost of experience isn't too high
Provided always you profit thereby.

Fluently Plausible
Suspect the plausible, smoothly fluent:
Their feigned reliance tends to play truant.

Focus
A luminary lights the way.
Beware! False focus leads astray.

Folly
At times when folly says insist,
You're better served if you desist.

Forgive
When people transgress and impose distress,
Forgiving, though hard, serves all of us best.

Future Pursuits
Refrain from pursuing great gains still to come:
In sprints to the future you're mostly outrun.

Gaffes
Though it's hard retracting the gaffes we make,
It has to be done for conscience's sake.

Gifts
Gifts after Christmas are half as dear,
So snap some up for birthdays next year.

Gratification
Don't hasten to shorten anticipation:
Delay increases your gratification.

Grievances
Grievances issue from something unfair;
If they're not settled, they turn to despair.

Heads I Win
Hearing 'Heads I win,' suspect a ruse.
Don't let it be said 'And tails you lose'!

Heat Loss Remedy
Two layers of paper and one of emulsion
Provide loss of heat with that simple solution.

Hidden Knowledge
Keep your knowledge, like cash, in your wallet;
Don't show it solely because you've got it.

High Regard
Remember the rule when you crave respect:
Never give anyone cause to suspect!

Irredeemable Pledge
If ever you feel you've arrived at life's edge,
Make for yourself an irredeemable pledge.

Jobs
Don't pack up your tools till you're sure the job's done;
There's always some battle before a war's won.

Know-alls
In conversations, let know-alls talk first:
They hate to hear their opinions reversed.

Know-alls' Lapses
The joy of a know-all is knowing a lot
Discounting, of course, the things they forgot.

Know-it-all
Let's contain our disdain for the know-it-all;
His presence can save a professional's call.

Lateral Thinking
In earnest pursuit of answers to questions,
It helps to explore far wider directions.

Laurels
Don't lie on your laurels. You never can trust
That doubts on your morals won't turn them to dust.

Linctus
When taking a linctus to stop you from coughing,
Try to think of a drink you'd rather be quaffing.

Listening and Talking
Increasingly listening your benefits soar:
For in talking much less you're bound to learn more.

Look Round
Take a look round before guests go away:
It won't be they who have carriage to pay.

Maybe
Do disputes arise between 'yes' and 'no'?
More using of 'maybe' might help, if so.

More Absorbing
Having started a novel and found it boring,
Persevere! It may make the next more absorbing.

Near Perfection
Seeking perfection's a valid intention
In striving to claim well-earned satisfaction.

Nettle Mettle
Taking a hint from the nettles I've grasped,
Never be tentative, feckless or last.

New Year
Each New Year gives us a fresh beginning
To make a life that's truly fulfilling.

Now's the Time
Don't reach the point where you wish you'd said it.
Speak out the words! Best heard, not regretted.

Parasites
It isn't everyone gives you your due:
Beware the parasites praying on you!

Plain Sailing
Though you're told that from here on its all plain sailing,
Ahead there's the chance of something that's failing.

Point-proving
When proving a point, refer to your source;
Otherwise, fiction's your only recourse.

Ponder the Options
Before deciding which route to take,
Your time's well spent if you hesitate.

Poor Counsel
Don't mountaineer till you've climbed a mountain:
Such mad advice makes progress uncertain.

Prior Consideration
A degree of discretion prior to action
Might serve to avoid an annoying infraction.

Prizes
If you want to walk off with all of the prizes,
Offer the judges some pleasant surprises.

Quality's Failure
At times when quality fails to deliver,
It needs to apply a little more rigour.

Quote
If someone happens to quote what you've said,
Don't let the flattery go to your head.

Racy Fun
The best advice if you only want fun,
Is not to bet till the race has been won.

Radiator
Where a radiator's attached to a wall,
To clean underneath it it needs to be tall.

Rainbow's End
Remember to nurture life's special friends:
You never can tell where the rainbow ends.

Reciprocity
Reciprocating a fellow's favour
Needn't make either lesser or greater.

Relaxation
Swallow life's pleasures like bolting your meals,
And miss the flavours relaxing reveals.

Remembering
Before posting things to your memory for good,
Be sure they've been stamped with the word 'understood'.

Remembering Dates
Never forget to remember a date:
Forgetting memories makes loved ones irate.

Respect
In dealings with others, you'll earn respect
When actions you take match those you'd accept.

Responsibility
Never consider responsibility
Referential to others exclusively.

Resting
Resting too much can lead to rusting:
So keep active and stay on existing.

Right for the Job
For all sorts of jobs it's important to choose
Which glues, bolts or screws are the right ones to use.

Risk Prediction
Risks are not things to be taken too lightly:
One needs to predict the outcome most likely.

Rogues
For the rogue proposing a change of heart,
Telling the truth is a great way to start.

Self-content
Replace your intention of heaping up wealth;
The way to contentment is sharing yourself.

Self-demeaning
Being tempted to mock, don't meanly deride:
It's you who's demeaned if you hurt someone's pride.

Self-enquiry
Question yourself before judging another,
Else relevant knowledge you mayn't discover.

Self-praise
Conceit's a trait requiring replacement
Acquired by practising self-effacement.

Shards or Sherds
Call it a shard or refer to a sherd:
Either will do, but the second's most heard.

Sinnings
The antidote to criminal sinnings
Is choosing a route to new beginnings.

Situations
When you're not quite sure of a situation
You can always ask for an explanation.

Snide Remarks
A snide remark within one's hearing
Won't make its sayer awfully endearing.

Solar Import
Making the most of what sunshine allows,
Ignore all displays of the floating clouds.

Spontaneous Succour
A reassuring, helping hand
Should be automatic, not planned.

Stagnation
A way of avoiding stagnation, you'll find,
Is having a project to challenge your mind.

Stick to Your Guns
He who decides to change his mind
Might feel he's left better behind!

Stressed
If you need to relax, start a new chore;
You'll soon feel less stressed than you were before.

Superstitions
It you're superstitious and also sober,
Don't ever ignore a four-petal clover.

Telephone's Ring
Beware the enticing telephone's ring:
You can't be sure of the news it might bring.

Talkative Women
Here's a piece of advice that women might heed:
After starting a sentence, they needn't proceed.

The Tempter
Decline any tempting offer of lunch;
Better go Dutch if it comes to the crunch.

Tempters
Should a tempter fail to obtain success,
Don't fail to obtain their contact address.

Tempting Distractions
Cling to the rapture as long as you can:
Distraction can tempt both woman and man.

Terminology
Odd terms that arise and appear confusing,
You're well advised to consider not using.

Testimonials
When testimonials enthuse us to buy,
We should stop and consider what catches the eye.

Theories
A surfeit of theories can clutter the mind,
So stick to the best and leave others behind.

Think Ahead
If nothing that's timely is tried or said,
It always pays to be thinking ahead.

Tiling
If the bathroom wallpaper starts to peel,
A bout of tiling might seem the ideal.

Tolerance
Though patience is held as a virtuous trait,
Beware its holder becoming irate!

Tomorrow
Should you finish today avoiding disgrace,
Tomorrow will start with a welcoming face.

Tomorrow Will Do
In case there's a matter you'd sooner eschew,
Remember the mantra: 'Tomorrow will do'.

Tomorrow's Yesterday
Today is tomorrow's yesterday;
Try to ensure that it earns its stay.

Tomorrows
Seek to discard the worst of your sorrows
And concentrate on better tomorrows!

Trunk Call
An elephant's trunk is very efficient;
Beware any logger who claims it isn't.

Twigs and Leaves
If only the twigs and leaves could talk,
We'd learn much more from taking a walk.

UV Rays
Defend yourself from UV rays
With lotions and protective sprays.

Visitors' Needs
When you entertain visitors on your TV,
You should try to find out what they'd most like to see.

Wisdom and Knowledge
Though knowledge is known to be universal,
Wisdom quite wisely remains strictly personal.

Wording
Don't hasten to change any wording you wrote:
You still might prefer what it was you first wrote.

Work Ethic
When problems or evils encumber one's mind,
Devotion to working soon puts them behind.

Worth Doing
When something needs doing, give it your best;
Otherwise, pass it to somebody else.

Wrongs
Better to right a wrong that's been done
Than make excuse for the wronged one to shun.

**

CHAPTER 47 with 238 two-liners

TO PONDER

Abstract Notions
Abstract notions are mostly theoretical:
Their partners, however, choose things more physical.

Alienation
The simplest hint of alienation
Invokes a feeling of isolation.

Ambition
Our every kind of want and need
Demands we on ambition feed.

Ambivalence
Power, once attained, can prove an illusion
Or might create a perfect solution.

Arranging Change
If only we could rearrange
The crazed disruptions of change.

Association
Nothing's considered in isolation:
Solace itself requires consolation.

Autodidact
His Oxford was avidly reading books;
His Cambridge the watching of crows and rooks.

Beggars
In various countries, the need to beg
Encourages larger families, it's said.

Being Licked
Envelopes shortly may disappear:
Email's the foe they've mostly to fear.

Best Defenders
Remember, when choosing pets to protect us,
The ugliest dogs are the best defenders.

Blunder
If ever you play into some man's hands,
You've only blundered if he understands.

Body and Mind
Swimming reveals a body's appeal:
Assessing a mind's a tad surreal.

Boring Glories
Endless boilings of personal glories
Precipitate bores from over-egged stories.

Bras
Unlike the cigar that's a threat, though inventive,
A bra can be pretty as well as preventive.

Bribery
Though a briber pays the price and loses face,
The one bribed must face the ultimate disgrace.

Cause for Support
It's mainly a cause whose future's unsure
Attracts one's support to remain secure.

Caution
Whenever caution is thrown to the wind,
Think what disasters such risking could bring.

Celebritation
They recycle their fame in another's domain
By displacing their reign with no semblance of shame.

Charisma
Charisma's so potent, its fascination
Inspires its victims' infatuation.

Chattering Classes
Often abusive, the chattering classes
Have great appeal for the nattering masses.

Ciphers
Words have meaning, minds have thoughts;
Ciphered wording thinking thwarts.

Clean Set
The words clean, cleaner and cleanest make a neat set;
Sensibly cleanse and cleanser have one they reject.

Coastal Attraction
The reason the seaside appeals to most people
Is its wide-open space where everyone's equal.

Comedy and Tragedy
Thinkers among us find living comedic,
Those fraught with emotion constantly tragic.

Common Sense
At times it's woefully hard to fathom
If common sense is really that common.

Compliments
She'll briefly assess each statement he spouts:
It's just his compliments bypass her doubts.

Concentration
Holding focus builds attention
Into stable concentration.

Confusion
What can emerge from a state of confusion
Is someone who spots a simple conclusion.

Congratulation
Whenever according congratulation,
We're tacitly showing our admiration.

Conscience
Whenever we risk committing offences,
Conscience will trigger our moral defences.

Consequences
A consequence follows from something before,
An outcome to favour or else to deplore.

Contradiction
Opposition's a case of contradiction
That often occurs between fact and fiction.

Conversing
Conversing involves a quantum of thought:
Gossip revolves around shopping or sport.

Correction
Proof of an error requires confirmation;
The relevant truth's enough explanation.

Corruption
When righteousness yields to evil's attraction,
Corruption receives its piece of the action.

Dawn's Yawn
After the night and before the morning
May be the moment when Earth is yawning.

Debaters
Locked in debate, lacking facts to hand,
They overstate what they understand.

Deconstruction
Smile at the pundits who analyse
The self same things others criticize.

Dependence
The future fashion of human toil
Depends on who'll be the last with oil.

Dereliction
Dereliction describes an abandoned state;
And even our duties can risk the same fate.

Despair
Despair is like sin without absolution,
Or hopeless patience that sees no conclusion.

Discipline
Disciples emulate leaders' roles:
Ultimate discipline heeds controls.

Discomfort
The smallest discomfort we suffer at home
Distresses us more than what tyrants condone.

Disillusion
Disillusionment ruins contentment:
Nothing stays new for more than a moment.

Distrust
Modest distrust could assist the prevention
Of utterly unexpected deception.

Doers and Don'ters
People who can, do for all of us:
Those unable to, practise on others.

Dogmas
Dogmas demanding pious adherence
Will surely yield to shame's interference.

Drop-dead Effect
If one's drop-dead gorgeous and both are alive,
Which one of those mortals expects to survive?

Due to Duty
It's utterly due to the dutiful classes
Directors sustain directorial status.

Eccentric
Eccentricity fashions the man
Who shies away from a central plan.

Effervescence
When effervescence has had its way,
Convalescence may come into play.

Envelopes
Out of the envelopes hitting the floor,
Those with a window we try to ignore.

Equality
The aim of equality never looks down:
Its envy is focused on higher renown.

Esteem
Esteem in which a person is held
May deviate from what is withheld.

Ever Present
Putting someone disliked clear out of your mind
Is really like meeting them daily, you'll find.

Exacting
Exacting a promise or retribution,
Itself can breed an exacting solution.

Exceptional Excellence
Excellence stems from what's exceptional,
Always deploring the detrimental.

Excessive Success
Excessively used, the word success
Reveals itself as pretentiousness.

Experts Exposed
When experts in discussion disagree,
What motivates their claims we plainly see.

Facts
Evasion of truth's a major problem:
Facts won't vanish because you ignore them.

Faded Beauty
An overblown rose is a pitiful belle;
Such beauty distressed sounds the solemnest knell.

Failure
Failure applies to the one who loses,
Not to the person whom fate abuses.

False Premise
An argument using a faulty assumption
Improbably reaches a proper conclusion.

Familiarity
Contempt isn't all familiarity breeds:
At producing people it frequently succeeds.

Fantasies
Though shadows create their own fascination,
It's objects that need your main concentration.

Fascination
Fascination spells enchanted attraction,
A state it shares with bewitching distraction.

Fates of Change
Change, by the fates' design, occurs
Like marriage - for better or worse.

Fear
Genuine fear the intrepid will credit;
Only the craven will claim they've not known it.

Fees
Something's that given, apparently free,
Given time enough accrues its own fee.

Fight and Delight
Life is a mixture of fight and delight:
One for the daytime, the other for night.

Flaws
Theories and diamonds are prone to be flawed,
And flaws are conditions that can't be ignored.

Forewarned
Those testing moments that make us quite scared
At least might leave us much better prepared.

Forgiveness
Seeking forgiveness, if rich or poor,
Mercy's the house with the open door.

Fortuity
Fortuity's role in plays of chance
Is serendipity's happenstance.

Frailty
When frailty's anxiety starts to appear,
The name of its trigger's undoubtedly fear.

Future's Appointments
Unspecified future soon loses the plot,
But with an appointment turns up on the dot.

Gagging with Ads
A state of affairs lacking means of redress
Is ad men gagging free speech in the press.

Generalization
Generalization frankly implies
The tacit telling of numerous lies.

Globalization
Any expansion of globalization
Is bound to increase dehumanization.

Good Luck
Unpredictable luck is a circumstance
Whose grand design will appear sometime, perchance.

Gossip
Tainted gossipers earn degrees
At universities of sleaze.

Habits and Myths
The rationalization of habits and myths
Is like disentangling our buts from our ifs.

Happiness
Logicians cannot account for happiness:
They just assume it's purely spontaneous.

Haste
Haste is renowned as a demon of speed.
It thereby excuses taking one's ease.

Having it Out
When having it out with a difficult person,
You're also releasing a pent-up aversion.

Heart Over Mind
The strength of mind on reasoning's part
Can not outsmart the stealth of the heart.

Honesty
Fame disdains the honest ordinary:
Life's sustained by basic honesty.

Hurt
How ironic it is that those we hold close
Are the selfsame ones who could hurt us the most.

If Only
Add every 'If only' to find the sum
Of human regrets that can't be undone.

Ignoring Dispute
Knowledge's course encounters dispute:
Ignorance favours an easier route.

Implementation
Thought and action, each on the other relies;
The artisan builds what the thinker contrives.

Improvement
You'll never improve if you're constantly praised;
Give critics a chance and you'll find you're amazed.

In Mind
Interpretation tries to find
What's in, or was in, someone's mind.

Induction
A formal admission defines an induction,
Accepting its partner's a glib introduction.

Inimical Jealousy
Enmity stemming from jealousy's greed
Will only lessen when threatenings succeed.

Insolence
Hurtful insolence bedevils the mind;
It's more to be pitied than be chastised.

Integrity
Integrity's demons, pride and pretence,
Need dedication to aid its defence.

Interruption
We can normally ride a brief interruption,
But that won't apply to a lengthy disruption.

Jostling
When people are jostling to get to the front,
It's always the elderly bearing the brunt.

Jug
If a jug's half empty it must be half full,
But if it gets broken the outcome's called null.

Lead and Feather
A morcel of lead and a like-weighing feather
Released side-by-side would make landfall together.

Leaders
A cult plays a leading role in culture,
While advent leads the way to adventure.

Levity
A modicum of levity
Might mitigate a tragedy.

Likelihood
Likelihood stretches from maybe to probably,
And beyond there some dodgy hints at certainly.

Managed Manners
Vaunted displays of impeccable manners
Are compromised when it's winning that matters.

Matches
Money and loving don't live together;
Giving and taking get along better.

Meditation
From meditation grows inclination,
Which flourishes on as firm intention.

Memory
Complete recall is what we lack;
Just certain things come swiftly back.

Mere Ideas
Don't blame an idea that leads you astray:
Ideas on their own don't have any say.

Mobile Morality
Reflecting change in societal thinking,
Ethical judgements are constantly shifting.

The Model
Making a model from many small parts
Leads one to ponder on nature's fine arts.

Modulation
Whilst one's tones submit to regulation,
Changes of pitch have their modulation.

Moments
A moment enjoys an unmeasured extent;
After sixty seconds, a minute is spent.

Monotony
Variety's repertoire daily increases;
Monotony constantly plays the same pieces.

Natural History
Natural history is hard to explain:
Nobody knows whence the history part came.

Nature's Balance
As tides in their ebbing and flow maintain,
One person's loss is another one's gain.

Nescience
Ignorance comes with a mental clean sheet
That knowledge, through time, might try to complete.

New Beginnings
Much can arise from lucid conclusions:
Endings often engender beginnings.

No Excuses
Do not allow freedom to make excuses
For letting yourself indulge in abuses.

No Promises
No dreamer may on sleep rely,
And sleep will often dreams deny.

Nobility
Nobility's notional obligations
Should show regard for plebeian aspirations.

Nothing New
Nothing is new throughout the whole world,
Only things hidden like flags unfurled.

Nothingness
Nothing extant can deny a beginning,
And no beginning arises from nothing.

Now
Like an anxious lover awaiting a suitor,
Today is the past's unforeseeable future.

Opinions' Origins
The stuff of which our opinions are made
Is the fund of thoughts our brains have conveyed.

Opposites
Simplicity stitches in sober lines:
Complexity weaves exotic designs.

Optimal
You can criticize what's deemed the optimal,
Only to find whatever's most favourable.

Originality
Originality doesn't invest
In ordinary shares of good common sense.

Origination
Inspiration will flow from outer creation:
Cogitation breeds inner origination.

Out of their Hands
When people pretend things are out of their hands,
Their pretences can vary like shifting sands.

Outside and In
Allusion's a reference to something else:
Illusion's a mystery in itself.

Over Wait
That thing for which you're willing to wait
Might just contrive to arrive too late.

Passing Days
Today we're immersed in hapless exertion;
Yesterday winged it in taskless desertion.

Passing Time
To pass the time we embark on some task,
Though time won't need us to help it to pass.

Pedant
The pedant who's constantly chasing facts
Ought on occasion to pause and relax.

Pedantry
Immersed in concerns to the utmost degree,
The pedant relieves us of stress we don't need.

Percipience
What's often called reading between the lines
Applies to those with percipient minds.

Perfection
We only know perfection's achieved
If the objective was earlier agreed.

Pivotal Moment
A pivotal moment can open our eyes
To envisage a scene where our future lies.

Poignancy
Surely one can't be instinctively sad;
Only some poignancy leaves one that bad.

Poor Benefit
Without poorer writing, composing and art,
We wouldn't know how to set better apart.

Postbags
Letters to papers are differently seen;
For most, they're a valve for letting off steam.

Postcodes
Local postcodes aren't so simple to break:
Take a near town's and not make a mistake.

Posterity
We work for a future our children deserve;
Posterity never reacts in reverse.

Practical Tenet
A practical tenet, one shortly discovers,
Is try to refrain from depending on others.

Preconception
The appearance of birth before conception
Only occurs perusing a lexicon.

Predicaments
Predicaments frequently trace their cause
To faulty predictions that staggered off course.

Prejudgment
It seldom pays to presume conclusions:
Guesses misplaced create false illusions.

Pretence
Ignorance commences where knowledge ends;
Unknowing ones then resort to pretence.

Priorities
Providing that goodness retains its place,
The pleasures of living reap no disgrace.

Processions
Processions parade for special occasions
Displayed by respective manifestations.

Produce and Consume
Leaving beaver lodges and bird nests excused,
Man alone will consume as well as produce.

Prognostication
It's known for a hopeless prognostication
To conjure the magic of realization.

Promisings
What looks promising warrants pursuing;
Anything promised should be ensuing.

Propaganda
Through propaganda, albeit untruth,
As in propagation something takes root.

Prophecies
Regardless of promises prophets contrive,
Remember the future will never arrive.

Psychiatrists
In preference to studying strippers and dancers,
Psychiatrists look to the audience for answers.

Psychological Time
Enjoying disporting, days seem shorter:
Quitting philandering, somewhat longer.

Punctuality
Punctuality's one of the surest signs
Of a soul in a desultory state of mind.

Quality
Disdaining thought of boring equality,
His aim in life was fostering quality.

Questions
Posing questions expressed with reticence
Promises answers brimmed with arrogance.

Rate of Change
Change's rate of acceleration
Leaves no space for consolidation.

Reactionaries
Openly favouring rigid conformity,
Reactionaries squander originality.

Realization
Imagination and science's fictions
Greet realization of their predictions.

Recall
Some things you've known once can be wretched to find
When deeply ensconced in the depths of your mind.

Recessional Option
It's bizarre that whenever recessions occur,
The inspector's preferred to the entrepreneur.

Reckless
The word reckless suggests
One cares nowt about wrecks.

Reflection
Unlike the mirror's instant reflection,
Our own proceeds from longer inspection.

Regression
Regression's regret's in
Its sense of direction.

Reluctance
Reluctance shuns immediate action:
Delay affords it more satisfaction.

Removal Days
Risk of loss when you move to new places
Hinges on what 'removal' embraces.

Reply Expected
While making a statement, it's hard to deny
The phrase 'isn't it?' clearly expects a reply.

Reseeding
Keep on sowing fresh seeds for germination:
Other life exceeds your own termination.

Resemblance
For resemblance to work, things need the same traits;
Too many discrepancies lead to mistakes.

Revenge
A lingering thought of revenge for wrongs
The process of healing sadly prolongs.

Rewards
Rewards for competence no one confirms:
Prominence promises safer returns.

Rights
Though glad when told we've been right all along,
We sadly neglect our right to be wrong.

Roving Planet
If you follow the route of a roving planet,
You might rapidly find it's the sun that planned it.

Safety
If safety comes first, then what comes second?
Keeping alert deserves to be reckoned.

Satire
Subtle satire will gently expose
A subject's vices somebody knows.

Scarcity
Scarcity rarely lowers the price:
The more there are, the less they entice.

Sceptics
Sceptics offer opinions we're likely to flout,
Leaving little to feed on but portions of doubt.

Screw-top Containers
Whether or not for medicinal pills,
Those round containers come only part-filled.

Second Thoughts
He never considered counting his thoughts,
Nor thought how seconds could earn their rewards.

Self-consciousness
Self-consciousness doesn't affect the rabbit;
In humans it's known as an abject habit.

Self-motivation
Failure's a favour we grant to ourselves;
Self-motivation its stigma dispels.

Sequents
Consequent knows it results from a cause:
Subsequent shows it's a matter of course.

Serendipity
Serendipitous occurrences
Prove fortuitous discoveries.

Shame
Truthful offenders exhibit more shame
Than perjurers who their untruths declaim.

Shared Secrets
A secret shared with a person now dead
Is safer by half than was formerly pledged.

Silence
Silence is peace that we shamefully shatter
Indulging in speech devoid of grey matter.

Silent Witness
A monument hasn't the means to repent
The message not it but its maker had meant.

So Far
What he meant when he uttered 'so far so good'
Was he'd finish the job, assuming he could.

Social Strata
A social stratum of overall competence
Sanctions the rest to indulge their insouciance.

Sounds
Sounds give emotions double their measure:
Moaning can come from grief and from pleasure.

Spare Me
Protect me, please, from the happy medium,
That telling synonym for tepid tedium!

Stability
When the wealth of the nation is stable at last,
Scant attention's addressed to the privileged class.

Stable Progression
The ladder of progress relies on old rungs
To carry the loading of those still to come.

Succession
A man's not honoured by being replaced;
Being succeeded's a different case.

Succinctness
Statements of fact abhor amplification;
What they prefer is succinct presentation.

Succour
Supplies provided to people in need
Could heighten their plight if ceased or retrieved.

Supernatural
Unravelling supernatural laws
Will bolster nature's terrestrial cause.

Superstitious Habits
Superstitions, like magic, are mere pretence:
Irrational tricks for imagined defence.

Suspicion
Achieving an influential position
Tends to initiate public suspicion.

Tastes in Life
Our tastes in life are seldom stable:
We undertake just what we're able.

Techno Folly
Whenever technology enters the fray,
Nature's faithful benefits wither away.

Temptation
Temptation assumes that you want what it's got;
It's you who decides if it's worth it, or not.

Thatcher
With powerful speech she conveyed her believings,
As Pisa's sloped tower displays its own leanings.

There and Back
Though both routes are the same, homeward journeys incline
To feel shortened by kind psychological time.

Thick as Bricks
They'll soon have bricked over the whole of the planet.
Whither the rain on drives and gardens, goddammit?

Think First
Good sense, one can say without doubting,
Is pondering prior to spouting.

Thrift
Thrift's a pink flower that grows on cliff tops
And gives a big hint to folk on the rocks.

Time
A sluice can slow a river's way,
But time will never brook delay.

Time the Healer
The steady effluxion of querulous time
Will soon find disputing in welcome decline.

Time's Measure
The passage of years can appear too fleet:
Time is the measure that foils such deceit.

Time's Tasks
Time is an implement poised to fulfil
The tasks that life can impose at its will.

Transgressions
Open admission of lesser transgressions
Parries the making of greater confessions.

Truisms
Uniquely a truism states the truth
Without requiring the usual proof.

Trust
Honoured canons and customs provide
A base where the soul of trust may reside

Trusting to Chance
In crossing your fingers you're trusting to chance,
But chance needn't heed such a weird circumstance.

Two Fingers
Two fingers denote a victory sign;
Their other roles need some cheek to define.

Ubiquitous Dawn
No place can proclaim their daybreak's unique:
Worldwide it's dawn every hour of each week.

Unheeded
When riots occur as the peace is disturbed,
We hark to the echoes of voices unheard.

Ups and Downs
More people talk of climbing a hill
Than those who think of descending will.

U-turn
A U-turn reversing a person's direction
Assumes an erroneous earlier intention.

Vacuums
No sooner a space is deprived of air,
Than nature attempts to divert some there.

Veiled Intention
Odd people receiving helpful attention
React by suspecting some veiled intention.

Vicarious Amends
When we seek salvation through medic or priest,
By our own atonement their burden's increased.

Vicious Circles
Don't fear the wrath of a vicious circle:
It mangles the mind, never the person.

Virtue's Values
Virtue's qualities cannot be shaken
By immorality's reputation.

Virtues and Vices
All the virtues and all the vices
Survive in part on compromises.

Vulgarity
Vulgarity comes with a natural licence
That hasn't been tempered by social politeness.

Water
Despite the free raindrops that fall from the sky,
Fresh water's a gift that we all have to buy.

The Way Things Are
It's easy to say 'that's the way things are':
Making them better is harder by far.

Weaknesses
In achieving a balance of give and take,
The weak concentrate on mistakes the strong make.

Wealth and Renown
Wealth and renown have similar aims:
Each to achieve its maximum gains.

Wedlock
Marriage can tease you if fretting with doubt
About life within and living without.

Wishing
Wishing mixes regret and frustration,
Both arising from spiteful temptation.

CHAPTER 48 with 38 two-liners

TRANSPORT

Aeroplanes
While it's common knowledge that aeroplanes fly,
Without puff or pilot they'd better not try.

Bicycles Reign
For enjoyment and health the cyclist maintains
The motor car tries, but the bicycle reigns.

Bike
Oh how we sang, my bike and I,
Our theatre the boundless sky.

Biking
A humble bike of the pedalling kind
Can rid your mind of the workaday grind.

Caravans
While caravans hamper, through lack of pace,
They equally challenge our waste of space.

Cars
Each day they make them larger and faster
In mindless haste towards oil-less disaster.

Commuting
A daily commute when traffic is bad
Could drive a man incrementally mad.

Cycling
Two wheels were always the socialist's ride;
Now bikes are used by all parties, with pride.

Damn and Blast!
A puncture is the cyclist's curse;
Only a chain-break could be worse.

Driveways
Where driveways to houses are made of gravel,
Pebbles in tyre-treads find journeys to travel.

Driving
The older you get the less you like driving;
No wonder, then, that the taxis are thriving.

Driving and Cycling
Driving is quite an expensive affair;
Cycling can find you with money to spare.

Healthy Bike
The bicycle remains by far
More healthy than the motor car.

Helicopters
With clattering rotors, their devilish plan
Is trying to make as much noise as they can.

Highway Drivers
When drivers on highways go too closely
At least they should learn to drive more slowly.

Kerbstones
Those diminutive carpark walls
Cause many pedestrian falls.

Locomotive
Spry noun 'locomotion' sounds more attractive
Than adjectival's shy 'locomotive'.

Mad Drivers
Although they can see a sharp corner's looming,
Mad drivers still keep their engines consuming.

Misty Landing
Through thick mist and hoping the runway's still there,
Primed pilots descend on a wing and a prayer.

Mobile Smiles
Personal number plates match one's style:
Preferred are those which raise a wry smile.

Motorbike Riders
A motorbike rider keeps twisting his wrist,
Consuming good petrol that soon won't exist.

Multiple Junctions
For overseas folk it's whether they dare,
While local drivers play devil-may-care.

Overcast
Apply the bike's brake that stops the front wheel
And receive a scar that's hard to conceal.

Proud Bikers
Motorcyclists who like their bikes over-loud
Seem to think extra noise can make them feel proud.

Public Transport
The so-called bus shelters scattered in town
Give scant relief when the rain's pelting down.

Residential
If you live in an area that's residential,
A regular bus is considered essential.

Reversing Noise
With a noisy pantechnicon always reversing,
The bulk of the neighbourhood's constantly cursing.

Riders
Riding pertains in the main to horses:
Cycling relies on human resources.

Riding Again
At seventy-six he's riding again,
Feet on the pedals both straining the chain.

Road Noise
Raucous old motors once caused all the noise;
Now it's the traction of tyres that annoys.

Roundabouts
A roundabout is alright for the deft;
They know to go right, you have to turn left.

Sequitur
As he drove a hard bargain and a large car,
One tends to suspect that connected they are.

Traffic Calming
Traffic calming through bumps and obstructions
Are frequently plagued by weird instructions.

Traffic Lights
Lights that change from red to green show red-plus-amber:
Those that change from green to red alone show amber.

Trailer Baby
Towing a trailer with baby inside
Isn't a chore, more a matter of pride.

Unfair Repairs
When the market for cars is hitting a low,
Your bills for repairs are a horrible blow.

Vanman's Mantra
My urgent plan's to get me there
From where I am, with time to spare.

A Wide Berth
As an anchored vessel needs space for its turning.
So cyclists deserve to be given wide berthing.

CHAPTER 49 with 25 two-liners

WAR

Acts of War
Companions in war do deeds, through compulsion,
That each at home would reject with revulsion.

Annexation
Annexation ignites
Territorial fights.

Armed Arbitration
Failing all peaceable disputation,
War's the notorious arbitration.

Confrontations
If earth possessed fewer rivers and mountains,
It's likely there'd be more peace between nations.

Diplomatic Warring
Diplomacy's notion is warring with words;
By copious nations that sort is preferred.

Endangerment
Mature generations that send us to war
Endanger the young, not consulted before.

Enmity
We're weary of hate and the wars that depress us.
May the end of enmity grace our successors!

Fortune
If fortune, as claimed, really favours the bold,
It plainly was absent from battles untold.

Hell
Could but the fallen have stories to tell,
The clearer the picture we'd have of hell.

Homage
We thank the Lord for the 'Hurry' and 'Spit'
And valiant pilots in flying kit.

It Takes a War
When a war is over, and our side won,
The folk from all classes join in the fun.

Kinsmen
Our kinsmen fought with peerless temerity,
Set on glory, ignoring longevity.

Make Do and Mend
Remember the saying 'Make do and mend'?
It helped us to win the war in the end.

Men of the Front
Old soldiers of the front, we honour them today:
All those who bore the brunt yet never fled the fray.

An Officer and a Lady
He rose for the lady despite his wound;
Perceiving his grief she instantly swooned.

Old Bowler
During Veterans' Day not a soul complained
Of the cap he wore where haircream once reigned.

Patriotism
To die for his land the patriot is willing,
But must understand it likewise means killing.

Privatized War
It might be the right thing to privatize war,
Although the wrong wages would probably soar.

Siren Time
With only shelters and tables for cover,
It had to be one, or if not, the other.

Taloned Threat
When doves of peace are torn to pieces,
The taloned threat of war increases.

Technology
Faced with war's needs for more lethal supplies,
The pace of technology can but rise.

Tragedy
Heroes have sensed where heroics were needed,
And sometimes not learning if they succeeded.

War
A war is where vast sums are made
Without some advertising aid.

Warriors
Mankind will never conquer war:
That's what man's warriors are for.

Wars
Through all the wars fought in the name of good,
More grief has been wreaked than ever it should.

CHAPTER 50 with 22 two-liners

WEATHER

British Weather
British weather constantly checks the sky,
Imposing changes that challenge the eye.

Bus-stop
Our bus-stop shelter placed close to the town
Gives scant protection when rain's pelting down.

Clouding
Clouds that cloak the sun make a bather shiver,
And when raindrops fall even more than ever.

Crampon Time
When ice occurs after earlier rain,
A vertical stance is hard to maintain.

A Choice of Weather
Sunshine at Christmas and snowflakes in June
Suggests that the weather can choose its own tune.

Christmas Gifts
Don't think of gloves, or a scarf, or a sweater:
Sunblock and sunspecs will cheer them up better.

Complaining
There's no point in complaining
Just because it starts raining.

Crampon Time
When ice occurs after earlier rain,
A vertical stance is hard to maintain.

Down to the Clouds
Not till the clouds have scurried away
Can gleaming sunbeams brighten the day.

Expressions
Like the expression on somebody's face,
The weather can change with unnerving haste.

Hiding Clouds
When I scan the blue sky I wonder where
All the clouds hide at such time as I'm there.

Impersonation
When rolling nimbus impersonates waves,
We can but wonder at nature's displays.

Mobile Clouds
Stand watching them as long as you will,
You'll seldom see clouds that are standing still.

Nature's Eye
The weather hourly paints the sky,
Detecting change through nature's eye.

Nature's Tenant
Climatic changes that seem to increase
Are nature's tenant renewing its lease.

Shower
Though artificial, a shower can play
The part of rain on the sunniest day.

Sun and Moon
As our orbiting sun dictates the weather,
The moon and the waves keep pulling together.

Sunshine
In cooler countries, among the temptations
Is chasing the sunshine's brief revelations.

Washing Watch
Alert to the weather, the launderer waits
To gather-in washing as raining dictates.

Weather Debate
Once released from the grip of night time's tether,
The English debate the state of the weather.

Weather Lore
Low pressure portends a spell of wet weather:
To keep it at bay, display your umbrella!

Weather Predicting
Weather predicting's a conjuring trick:
It won't matter much which option you pick.

CHAPTER 51 with 82 two-liners

A
BONUS MISCELLANY

Towels
Should you hang a towel on the bathroom door,
There's a risk it will drop and jam on the floor.

Appropriate
Whenever 'appropriate' fits the bill,
'Suitable' has the same role to fulfil.

Dawn
When the sun announces a crimson dawn,
We feel that a happy day has been born.

Chocolates
After the feasting, the wine and the beer,
Boxes of chocolates are next to appear.

Courting
Courting's a feature of most people's years:
It either succeeds or ends up in tears.

Vacations
Vacations, like minutes, use the same knack:
Once you have had them you can't take them back.

Brushing and Touching
When just passing, two people might brush:
If even closer, they're likely to touch.

Nightjars
Churring nightjars are secretive birds,
They fly at night when they can't be observed.

Plugs and Cables
With plugs and cables all over the place,
Rooms can sometimes look an utter disgrace.

Paintings Displayed
It's great to see your own paintings displayed:
You just have to hope their pigments don't fade.

Trash Cans and Bins
What a Yank calls a trash can a Brit calls a bin:
Still, both agree it's a thing we put rubbish in.

Unreliable People
There are certain people you can't rely on,
Often ones that you need to keep your eye on.

Turning Up
When people turn up without being invited,
There may be good reason for getting excited.

Repeats
Innumerable people sit glued to their seats
Combing TV programmes for decent repeats.

Envelope Problems
Black ink on red envelopes can make it too hard
For the Christmas postie to deliver each card.

Special Occasion
An event that's deemed a special occasion
Will often give rise to a celebration.

Native Villages
Native villages with cobblestone roads
Are always sought as holiday abodes.

Don't and Won't
Far too many say they will then they don't,
And even more strongly say that they won't.

Dressing-Down
After receiving a sharp dressing-down,
Getting dressed up you're the smartest in town.

Raindrops on Windows
Big raindrops on windows
Show which way the wind blows.

Sacking
It's not very nice to give someone the sack,
But there's much more pleasure in having them back.

Wood and Nails
While our neighbour buys wood and boxes of nails
We'll be glad when he stops what his banging entails.

Plumber
For water or heat refer to a plumber,
They'll fathom things out one way or another.

Toddlers
Toddlers are kids who've just started walking;
And, looking ahead, they'll never stop talking.

Combis and Boilers
Now the plural of combi is commonly used,
It's clear that with boilers we can't be confused.

Early Music
Listen to music when you get out of bed
And you won't be glum, you'll feel happy instead.

Older Swearing
The older you get you're more likely to swear,
Like a worn out rug that's in need of repair.

Number Ten
In London's Downing Street at Number Ten,
It's ten to one someone needs a new pen.

Creaking Hinges
When the hinge on a door begins to creak,
All you need's an oilcan within your reach.

Tea Bags
Soggy tea bags in teapots, it's not disputed,
Must have let the contents become too diluted.

Chocs and Swigs
People who daily have chocolates to eat
Make swigs of gin their occasional treat.

Postman
We once had a postman who'd stop for a chat,
But the need for speed put an end to all that.

Worm's Mistake
While watching a thrush as you lean on your rake,
You might see a worm make a vital mistake.

Discovering Honesty
One way to discover if someone's honest
Is finding they've done all the things they've promised.

Shadier Places
When you sit outside with the sun in your face,
You'd do better to move to a shadier place.

Prostitution
Prostitution, some say,
Is true love but with pay.

Wordsworth
How lucky was Wordsworth not watching TV,
Just having daffodils to go out and see.

Bats
Our bats have partners
That fly in darkness.

Plugs and Plugholes
You can have a plughole along with a plug,
But one or the other won't do any good.

Trimming for Visitors
When expecting visitors at the front door,
Make sure things are looking more trim than before.

Hedgehog
Every night the hedgehog returns to its hide
And settles the prickles on which it's relied.

Jupiter
Assuming that Jupiter's high in the sky,
There's really no chance of it landing nearby.

Tanner
A tanner is one who tans animal hides,
And as payment it's worth six pennies besides.

Blithering Pest
A brilliant idea that someone suggests
Can turn out to be a blithering pest.

Sticky Stamps
For very good reason
Stamps have strong adhesion.

Hair Trimming
Trimming your hair's nothing to do with your health,
Just one of those things you can't do for yourself.

Getting Annoyed
There are things in life that we try to avoid,
And one of them's actually getting annoyed.

Towers
When a tower's very tall
It looks likely to fall.

Angle Grinders and Drills
Hating the din of drilling and angle grinders,
We long for the day when we've left them behind us.

Wartimes
Since ancient days when fighting occurred,
We've never learnt that wars are absurd.

Parched
No matter wherever they happen to be,
Parched people may stop for a nice cup of tea.

Well Bedded
After the daffodils have been deadheaded,
It's for all of the rest to be well bedded.

Violin
Before starting to play the violin,
He shaved the bristles from under his chin.

Adoption
Before putting children up for adoption
Their parents should scan every possible option.

Guilt or Gilt
A porker has nothing to do with guilt,
It's just a young sow people call a gilt.

Knickers in a Twist
Whether you're mad or upset, you'll still persist
In saying your knickers are all of a twist.

Mayor and Mayoress
After the Mayor had quaffed a bottle of whisky,
It was said the Mayoress had turned equally frisky.

Skipper Aboard
Once the skipper's aboard
Flags just can't be ignored.

Rubber Bands
He's one of those fellows who never understands
How clever people can make such good rubber bands.

Easter Daisies
At Easter time dainty daisies are found
While around them pretty dewdrops abound.

Bringing the Bacon
The old saying 'to bring home the bacon'
Meant earning cash, if I'm not mistaken.

Culinary Needs
Parsley, mixed spice and various seeds
Meet some of the cook's culinary needs.

Speechifying
If you've planned a speech and have to present it,
Your listeners might wince if it's elongated.

Spires
At one end of the village there stands a fine spire,
While that at the east end is several feet higher.

Minding Your Business
If there's something special that hopes for forgiveness
It must be forgetting to mind your own business.

Historical Poems
Always having an eye on castles and ruins,
No wonder he took to historical poems.

Trees and Flowers
From the tallest of trees to the tiniest flower,
People sit and peruse them for many an hour.

Apple-pickers
In autumn the orchards' over-weight trees
Can bring apple-pickers down on their knees.

Billiards
Billiards allows just two balls in a game,
Unlike all of those that snooker can claim.

Chess
Some hobbyists get quite attached to chess,
Though the game is hard, one has to confess.

Puppet Show
When worked by the strings of a marionette,
The puppet show's something that kids don't forget.

Acclimatization
After people have moved to a new location
They'll be in some need of acclimatization.

Winter Clothing
As winter clothing begins to be shed,
Attractive chicks start looking ahead.

Notions
Those notions arising from some inclination
Will be of no use without implementation.

Photos in Albums
Photos in albums bring memories back
Of earlier games we used to enact.

Soup
With their meats and veggies both skirting the truth,
Broth always appears to be thicker than soup.

Tiles
Tiles on a wall
It's hoped won't fall.

Carpentry
The role of a carpenter seems to be
Reforming the shapes of wood from a tree.

Wheelibins
The use of wheelibins fosters recycling,
Reducing the level of landfill blighting.

England's Beauty
England's beauty once ranged from coast to coast;
Now, that's an ever-diminishing boast.

Peaks
The most majestic mountains are found
Where reaching peaks shake hands with the clouds.

Zips
Provided they always close and then open,
Zips will be known for reliable motion.

FINIS

www.ingramcontent.com/pod-product-compliance
Lightning Source LLC
Chambersburg PA
CBHW032100090426
42743CB00007B/181